ART

PAUL CÉZANNE
by Gerstle Mack

" It is the most complete biography I know, and probably the most complete in existence of the greatest artist of modern times; it is thorough and intelligent. . . . It is workmanlike and bears every mark of painstaking reliability." — Walter Pach

RENOIR: An Intimate Record
by Ambroise Vollard

" M. Vollard's book is a model of how such a thing should be. . . . It is a book packed with good stories. Every lover of personalities, every lover of pictures, and every art student should get hold of it." — J. Middleton Murry

These are Borzoi Books, published by
ALFRED A. KNOPF

MY FATHER
PAUL GAUGUIN

C

PORTRAIT OF HIMSELF
1888

MY FATHER

PAUL GAUGUIN

by

POLA GAUGUIN

Translated from the Norwegian by Arthur G. Chater

NEW YORK · ALFRED · A · KNOPF

1 9 3 7

ACKNOWLEDGMENTS

Certain of the material contained in this volume originally appeared in *The Intimate Letters of Paul Gauguin,* translated by Van Wyck Brooks, and issued by the Liveright Publishing Corporation; and in *Letters of Paul Gauguin to Georges Daniel de Monfreid,* translated by Ruth Pielkovo, published by Dodd, Mead & Company, to both of which publishers acknowledgment is made.

PREFACE

I AM the son of Paul Gauguin and a mother brought up in good bourgeois surroundings. In her home I grew up and predictions as to my future were many and various, ranging from solicitous doubts of how I might turn out, being the son of my father, to the somewhat too facile but dubious renown his name brought me later. A purely external resemblance in appearance and manner intensified the opinions people formed about me. The mystery which surrounded father's existence during my childhood and even in my adolescence was of great significance — a mystery which was deepened every time a letter came from him to mother; missives from far away, which for a little while rendered the strong and ever active woman silent and reflective. We children, without being told what was in these letters, instinctively felt the weight and significance of the words, and with the aid of the pictures we had at home, to us so familiar, to others strange, we freshened up

the image of him derived from a short visit he paid to Denmark when I was barely seven — a memory which remains with me to this day, clear and vivid as ever. Even now I recall with surprise how strange his language and his manner then seemed to me. That this was a father was something that was quite beyond my comprehension. The image has grown ever clearer and more alive with the passing of years. But it is always the same — just as he stood there, reserved, short-spoken, but moved, in the presence of his youngest son, whom he did not know and who, as he was aware, could not understand him — so do I see him still, the grown-up man, the stranger, Paul Gauguin, my father.

But the impression was sharply defined on the child's retina and gave him a feeling for every little thing which might in any way concern his father's life and work. Every idle word and every grain of gold that was let fall in connection with his name was gathered up and preserved. And the exclamation one heard so often: " Why, you're just like your father! " bound one closer to the image and set off its character; even if at times it retreated into the obscurity of the subconscious, it invariably returned each time to the light of consciousness, clearer, stronger, and more penetrating. No doubt while I was a child and right up to my father's death, when I was twenty, it was a fancy portrait, based on a few facts only. But the picture was a consistent whole. Then the

facts were added. First his two books, *Noa-Noa* and *Avant et Après*, with the commentaries I was able, as a grown man, to coax out of my mother. Commentaries that were remarkably clear, impartial, and revealing, supported by an excellent memory and stirred by a powerful but cool temperament, interspersed with a good deal of wit and humour and much practical self-esteem, born of family pride and ambition. But they were accompanied by a very human and frank understanding of the man to whom she had borne five children. She knew and respected the talented and industrious bank clerk she had married, appreciated his practical sense and many-sided ability, admired and was not a little proud of his health and strength. But Gauguin the artist was a stranger to her, and she never learned to understand this side of him.

It was beyond her comprehension that a man of his gifts and qualifications should take up anything so aimless as the career of an artist.

After reading Jean de Rotonchamps's and Charles Morice's biographies, which, by the way, give very different accounts of Gauguin's character both as man and as artist, mother decided that they gave no true portrait of him as a man; and in Somerset Maugham's novel *The Moon and Sixpence* she did not find a single trait of Strickland which had anything at all in common with her husband. Gauguin's published letters to Daniel de Monfreid aroused

pity in her without changing her view and without throwing any shadow over father's letters to her. Shortly before her death she gave me these letters: " Read them and they will give you a fairer estimate of your father; publish them if you think fit. He was a strong man both in his disposition and in his actions, without malice or suspicion. Perhaps he was rather inconsiderate in his candour and in acting according to his convictions, but he was always calm and consistent, without fanaticism. I could not understand his taking up art, though now I understand that he had a right to act as he did. But surely no one can be surprised that I refused to accompany him and bear him more children in an existence which to my mind was a mad and hopeless adventure."

To me these letters, together with an intimate study of his art, have been a valuable help in completing the image of Paul Gauguin which has followed and haunted me all through my youth and also to some extent during my subsequent career as an artist.

Besides the books mentioned above I have been much assisted by Frederick O'Brien's *White Shadows in the South Seas* and by conversations with some of father's friends, in particular the French sculptor and ceramic artist Paco Durio. These have been of great importance not merely as affording authentic information regarding definite events of father's

life, but also in helping me to understand the surroundings in which he lived.

What those who were directly associated with
him have to say of him as a man is of so conflicting
a character that I am convinced his feeling was introspective and that underlying it was a very strong
emotional life which did not easily find expression
in everyday intercourse.

And again his image is brought before me as I saw
him face to face for the first and last time, the son in
the presence of the father.

Years have passed, facts have accumulated, and
one's own experiences of life have explained much.
The father I did not understand as a boy of seven
has become Paul Gauguin, and when I attempt to
draw his portrait it is not the son that loved his father
who is writing, but myself, whose eyes have been
opened to Gauguin as artist and man by experience of
art gathered in the course of a life devoted to art and
determined by its conditions. Many inner voices,
good influences and bad, have combined to lead me
into the right way.

ILLUSTRATIONS

— *xiii* —

— xiv —

ILLUSTRATIONS

MY FATHER
PAUL GAUGUIN

⚉

CHAPTER 1

On the wall of No. 56 rue Notre Dame de Lorette, Paris, is a tablet recording that here on June 7th, 1848 the painter Paul Gauguin was born. There is nothing in the street, which resembles all other Paris streets, nor in the grey house itself to emphasize the significance of this piece of information. And were it not for the date an average observant Parisian would be unlikely to pay much attention to the tablet.

While the revolutionary date, June 7th, 1848, is written in letters of blood telling of the vain heroism in which many a bright young life was suddenly extinguished for the sake of an idea, the name of Gauguin is still traced in uncertain characters in the history of France. That it is found there at all and is likely to shine on with increasing lustre is due to Eugène Henry Paul, who saw the light of day at the very hour when the first gunfire rattled the windows of an ordinary prosperous apartment house in the rue Notre Dame de Lorette.

His father, Clovis Gauguin, came of a middle-class shopkeeping family in Orléans with pronounced republican views, as a result of which young Clovis took to politics in the turbulent years around 1830 and became a political contributor to the *National*. He did not attain to any great eminence as a political journalist, but in 1851, when Louis Napoleon made his *coup d'État*, his republican attitude forced him to go into exile with his family, consisting of his wife, Aline Marie, their five-year-old daughter, Marie, and their son, Paul, aged three. They were bound for Peru, where his wife had influential relatives. He died of a heart attack during the voyage and found his grave in the Straits of Magellan.

We are only able to draw a faint outline of Paul Gauguin's father and his father's family and of the influences he may possibly have had on his son's character. We may suggest a straightforward independence on a background of bourgeois liberalism. Perhaps we may also point to the impetuous optimism of an honest conviction, giving way to disappointment and depression in unreflecting moments. There are many indications that his intense preoccupation with recent events in Paris and his restless desire to reach Peru after the long voyage in a slow ship with an irritable captain were contributory causes of his sudden and early death. Impatient and short of breath he paced the deck, twenty-three steps

forward and twenty-three back, while his little son stood looking out over the vast expanse of the ocean and filling his lungs with the fresh sea breeze, which he was never to forget. When land was sighted the boy asked: " Papa, is that Peru? " — " No, my boy, we are scarcely half-way there."

Our information regarding Aline Marie and her family is more ample and definite, at any rate on her mother's side. Of her father, who was a wine merchant of Bordeaux named Chazal, we know little beyond that he was sentenced to twenty years' hard labour for having seriously wounded in a fit of jealousy his wife, Flora Célestine Thérèse Henriette Tristan, his marriage with whom had been dissolved eighteen years previously after a conjugal life of three years. Flora Tristan was no ordinary woman. She was born in Peru in 1803, daughter of a Spanish-Peruvian officer and nobleman, Don Mario Tristan y Moscoso, and a French lady. According to authentic reports the Moscoso family can trace their pedigree to the Borgias d'Aragon, and there is reason to think that they came to Peru, if not with Pizarro himself, immediately after he had made the country a Spanish province. Indeed, there are many traits in Gauguin's exterior and in his character which point to an admixture of Indian blood in the Moscoso family at some period. An old daguerreotype in the possession of the family, of a woman said to be a sister of Don Mario, makes this even more prob-

able. And there is no attempt to conceal it. On the contrary, Paul Gauguin, if the idea had occurred to him, would have been just as proud of this descent as he was of being a Borgia. He had no racial prejudices. He says himself: " Memoirs! They are history. Everything in them is interesting except the author. And he has to tell you who he is and where he comes from. Confessions! A serious business, according to Jean Jacques Rousseau. If I were to tell you that on the distaff side I am descended from a Borgia d'Aragon, Viceroy of Peru, you will certainly say I am boasting; but if I say we are a family of tramps you will look down on me. If I tell you that on my father's side we are all called Gauguin, you will say this is obvious naïveté, and if I go into details to prove I am no bastard, you will certainly smile at me."

And a little later Gauguin adds, now rather more directly and impulsively: " As you see, my life has been pretty stirring all through. There are many cross-currents in me. A coarse sailor-man? — if you like. But there is race in me, or, rather, there are two races."

At the age of fifteen Flora Tristan came to France and was married to Chazal in the following year. But humdrum married life did not satisfy her active spirit and certainly not her ambition. Peruvian romance, the romance of the Incas, was in her blood. Three years after her marriage she managed to get

a divorce so as to be able to devote herself entirely
to her own individual interests. Having made the
acquaintance of Père Enfantin she fervently em-
braced the Saint-Simonian doctrine, made her appearance as a journalist, wrote two novels, and did
not shrink from standing up at public meetings and
taking the part of the workers, not only in France
but also in England. Being pretty and temperamental, with a certain primitive and simple way of
expressing herself, she had no difficulty in attracting
attention. And even after the split in the Saint-Simon
circle she and Père Enfantin continued their agitation for social ideas and together founded a workers'
union in Bordeaux. The severe sentence passed on
her former husband gives us a hint that in spite of
her views, then regarded as subversive, and of her,
for a woman, somewhat irregular way of life, she
was able to surround her person with sympathy and
respect even in high places. Youth and charm and
an unconstrained eagerness produced a peculiar atmosphere about her, in which she was able to assert
her personality without having to consider public
opinion and could move among people of all classes
without having to produce evidence of her position
in order to uphold her dignity. Her own nature was
her best protection. She was not rich, could hardly
be called well off, but she was never at a loss when it
was a question of finding means for carrying on her
altruistic work for a cause which she believed to be

for the good of humanity. She died at the age of forty-two and the workers erected a monument over her grave in Bordeaux.

Her daughter, Aline, resembled her mother outwardly, was perhaps even prettier, as a certain feminine reserve added calm to her bearing and balance to her manner. To this her upbringing certainly contributed. She seldom saw her mother, occupied as the latter always was with meetings and lecture tours, and yet she was undoubtedly far more attached to her than to her father, feeling instinctively how profound and dangerous was the gulf which separated these two human beings. Her eyes were opened at an early age to the danger of impulsive acts, and her father's catastrophe, when she was scarcely twenty, intensified this. She only acted when obliged thereto by fateful circumstances. She was proud, tender, and kind, and held fast to what it was her duty to protect. She made no fuss and did not give way under the burden. She acted calmly and harmoniously according to her nature, but at the same time without calculation. Her son Paul understood this.

" How pretty and charming my mother was when she wore her Lima dress! Her face was half covered by the silk mantilla so that only one eye could be seen. An eye that was gentle and commanding, pure and caressing."

At an early age her mother placed her in a pension in Paris which was visited by literary men and

journalists of radical opinions, and here she met Clovis Gauguin, whom she married shortly after Flora Tristan's death. In all probability the latter, who at her divorce was not altogether without means, had had to settle a sum of money on her daughter, and Gauguin, as the eldest son of a prosperous tradesman's family, was certainly well enough off even during his father's lifetime to justify their establishing themselves in an apartment suited to a well-to-do Parisian bourgeois family.

And in fact three portraits painted by a friend of the house, Jules Laure, when Paul was about two years old, tell us of a happy young mother with two healthy and pretty children; a well-dressed little girl with her rather unmanageable curls charmingly arranged and a pair of lively brown eyes, and a blue-eyed boy with reddish hair at the age when one is painted without any clothes. Both pictures in oval gilt frames ornamented with stucco garlands and ribbons.

The portrait of their mother is a rectangular three-quarter-length representing Madame Gauguin seated in a gilt armchair upholstered in red plush. She is in a simple black velvet gown with white ruches at the wrists and at the slightly open throat. She is a good-looking woman of delicate build; in particular the painter has sought to emphasize the narrow, graceful, and shapely hands. While not remarkable as art, these portraits have an inti-

macy about them. They bear the impress of the painter's delight in his good models and tell us, as such portraits often do, more about the model's external traits and surroundings than about more personal qualities. What they reflect is the comfort of the home, its protective warmth.

The sudden breaking up of this cosy and comfortable home must have affected the young mother deeply, but perhaps the shock was mitigated by the thought of joining that side of her family of which she had been able to speak without difficulty and which was invested with a certain glamour of romance. Perhaps that would explain something of the exotic in her own nature, which her husband must also have remarked. But his sudden death upset all her prospects for the future, leaving her at once deserted and homeless. With only her two children she was now to land on foreign soil, to seek refuge with her family, who were nevertheless complete strangers to her, and without the husband who had given a meaning to her existence.

With him she might have built up a new home and held her own in the eyes of her relations. Alone with two children she was only a poor widow taking refuge with her rich family, at whose head was an aged man and among whom she would be treated with pity.

But in reality it turned out otherwise, thanks to the aged Don Pio. In spite of his hundred and seven

years he was a vigorous and genial man who kept a
large and hospitable establishment in Lima. He took
at once to his brother's grand-daughter with her
youthful charm, so that in a very short time she
occupied a leading place in the numerous family
circle. To her, coming from a simple bourgeois home
life, there was something fantastic in suddenly finding herself the centre of a family representing several
generations, which upheld its traditions in a manner
of life to her meaningless and extravagant. But whenever with her French tendency to reality she tried
to get firm ground under her feet, she felt herself a
stranger and not her own mistress. She became aware
of her dependence on this family with its primitive
joy in wealth, denying itself nothing, but jealously
guarding what was its own. In spite of the bond of
relationship she was the born Parisienne, to whom
her Spanish relatives showed the most exquisite
politeness, which in those of her own age took the
form of assurances of friendship — assurances, however, which were not backed by any great degree of
cordiality and which had to be renewed from day
to day if they were not to be forgotten. She must
assuredly have been homesick for France, especially
when thinking of her children's future.

To them life in Lima was a continual fairy-tale,
particularly for Paul, who had awakened to consciousness in a place where the sense of vision was
all-important. In Lima at that time, where monkeys

were the commonest domestic animals and where the vultures fought every evening over the offal of the streets, there was plenty to occupy a little boy whose greatest delight even then was to go out by himself in search of adventures, when he succeeded in eluding the watchfulness of his imperious elder sister. Where the children were concerned their mother regarded the future with something like anxiety. The boy was actually French, eldest son and, as his father's brother Isidore was unmarried, sole heir to the name of Gauguin; it was therefore quite natural to Aline Gauguin to undertake the long and troublesome voyage back to France, when after having lived four years in Peru she was informed of her father-in-law's death. As a French mother she knew her duty; she took the children with her, acted promptly, but unpractically. When Don Pio died in the following year, his will provided for a very liberal annuity for his ward; but the powerful family got the provision annulled and offered instead a smaller sum, which Aline Gauguin curtly refused. As we see, a proud and authoritative woman, but in a way weak. She did not protest, did not assert her right, but accepted what fate offered, and adjusted herself accordingly. The legacy she received from her father-in-law was a modest one, far too small to allow her to settle in Paris, as she would have preferred. In accepting the offer of her brother-in-law Isidore to share the old and spacious family house in Orléans

GAUGUIN'S MOTHER

TAHITI, 1892

ÉMILE SCHUFFENECKER AND HIS FAMILY
1888

she would be able to give her children a suitable education; there would be a small sum to start Paul in life and a dowry for her daughter, Marie.

This was the home in which Paul Gauguin passed his childhood up to the age of seventeen. Its head, Isidore Gauguin, was a confirmed bachelor, amiable and placid as could be, but without any pronounced qualities or interests; his familiar name, Uncle Zizi, gives us on the whole a kindly picture of the man. In the morning he was the attentive, sedentary tradesman, in the evening he pottered about his large garden. A radical in his political views, liberal-minded in religion, without fanaticism, he felt no craving to assert these views publicly nor did he seek any large circle of acquaintance which would permit him to do so. A dapper little man, he enjoyed the comforts of his home, paid his pretty sister-in-law the respectful homage she deserved, was grateful for the calm and simple manner in which she conducted the house, and took pleasure in the little sensations the children brought into his life, as a diversion in the big, quiet house. As a character Aline was entirely superior to him, and in a way she brought more colour into the middle-class home. She had literary interests, drew and painted in water-colour, and was also a good deal occupied with politics, but she had the profoundest distrust of everything which had to do with money and business. She would flare up angrily on noticing any symptoms of

a trading instinct in her son. Yet the tragic events she had witnessed in her father's case, her mother's unfettered outward activities, her husband's sudden death, and the four years of stirring, vivid, and exotic, but by no means intimate experiences in Peru had checked in a way her desire to assert herself and made her apathetic towards what went on outside this home, which was not her home.

For Petit Paul, as he was called, this home had no great attraction, in spite of his affection for his mother; and his impulsive, ever active, and intriguing elder sister Marie had sufficient eloquence and vigour to tyrannize over both her mother and him, in spite of her being only two years older. It was not altogether without reason that he was called Petit Paul. Throughout his childhood he was small and delicately built, physically backward, rather taciturn, as a rule very tractable, almost meek; but when he really set himself against a thing, he was obstinate to the point of stubbornness. He was not given to calculation in order to obtain an advantage, and he was inclined to be confiding, which made him an easy dupe. If he had won any advantage, his mother and sister were down on him, the latter to snatch it from him, the former because she considered it a reprehensible action. Little incidents which stick in the memory and acquire significance.

" One day I came home with some coloured glass marbles. My mother asked me angrily where I had

got them. I felt ashamed and told her I had swopped my rubber ball for them.

" ' I see, my boy, you've been doing business.'

" Business in my mother's eyes was a thing to be ashamed of. Poor mother! She was wrong, and yet she was right in this sense: that it taught me even as a child that there are certain things one does not sell."

During his first years in his uncle's home at Orléans there was one picture in particular which excited his imagination. It was an engraving of a traveller with a bundle on his back sauntering along the high-road, careless and unconcerned, in a beautiful sunny landscape. Its title, in ornate lettering, was *The Merry Wayfarer*. One fine day Paul set out cheerfully on the road with a bag full of sand hanging on a stick over his shoulder, turning his back on his home and its petticoat government. Towards evening he was picked up by the kindly butcher and brought back. His mother's sudden anger with the accompanying box on the ears from a by no means soft hand, her subsequent joy and tenderness, quenched for a long time his desire for adventure. But the tender restraint with which a mother surrounds a boy's craving for liberty often checks his fearless development more than a father's severe and tangible measures. It binds him more strictly in evoking his chivalrous instincts; the breaking of its bonds results in mental suffering, a sense

of guilt which is stronger than the feeling of physical pain one risks by trying to escape from the grasp of a father.

And for this reason it was his school that did more to develop the boy's character and open his eyes to human qualities, even if this came about in a manner different from that which was intended. At any rate, he tells us in after years:

" I won't say like Henri Régnier that this education did nothing for my mental development; on the contrary, I believe it did a good deal. Speaking broadly, I believe it was here I learned at an early age to hate hypocrisy, false virtue, and sneaking (*semper tres*), learned to distrust everything that was opposed to my instincts, my heart and my reason. I also learned there not a little of Escobar's spirit, which is certainly not to be rejected as an auxiliary. I acquired the habit of concentration and of continually watching my teachers' game. I taught myself to make my own playthings, as well as my own troubles, with all the responsibilities they involved.

" But this is a special case; in general I expect there is danger in the experiment."

Paul cannot have been particularly happy at school, but at any rate it never caused him much difficulty. He was apt rather than eager to learn, had no special abilities which he was trying to develop. And his mother had no special desires for his future beyond the negative one that he was not

to inherit the Gauguin family business in the little town of Orléans. The life she had been accustomed to, the traditions of her own family, obscure as they might be, made other claims and aspired to higher and more spacious things than were aimed at in Uncle Zizi's home.

And Paul himself instinctively felt that outside the narrow walls of this home there were things that had a message for him, demanding that he should liberate himself from mother, sister, and Uncle Zizi. He did not know what these things were, could not explain them. But he had once looked out over an ocean. As a boy of sixteen he was still physically backward and in spite of his observant and inquiring intelligence had difficulty in standing up to his mature and temperamental sister Marie. A certain boyish shyness of her womanly charm, and the feeling of chivalry which his mother by her whole nature evoked in him, almost always prevented him from having his own way. But this petticoat government worried him and he longed to get away from it.

For the son of a good family it was at that time a natural course to apply for admission to the Naval College. But his desire of travel was too great, and the actual goal too obscure, to allow him to concentrate on the subjects required for the entrance examination; so at seventeen it was decided that he should go to sea at once, with a view to becoming an officer in the merchant service.

It was with a certain surprise that Tombard, a kind and genial quadroon, captain of the *Luzitano*, received his new apprentice Paul Gauguin, a little slender-limbed lad, rather embarrassed by his new position as the youngest hand aboard a fine, well-found sailing-ship of 1,200 tons, which was to carry cargo and passengers between Havre and Rio de Janeiro. But he was dominated within by the thought of the adventures awaiting him — a thought which was connected with his childish memories of the ocean and of the country beyond it.

The day before they sailed he had a visit from the former apprentice, who brought him a card and a letter, asking him to deliver it at the address given and explaining that it would introduce him to a charming lady. The address was: Madame Aimée, Rua do Ouvidor.

This gave him something new to look forward to. The ocean voyage had a goal which meant something to him personally. Every forward movement of the vessel had its object, which he observed with interest. He felt himself growing, awakening as it were to the consciousness of a future. It was no longer a dream; life was under way. He gave little thought to the direction it might take, he only felt that it would lead somewhere. Favoured by the weather, the *Luzitano* carried him along to a foreign port and new surroundings. And one fine day the vessel anchored in Rio harbour, where she was to lie for a

month. A month which gave Paul, in Aimée's society, every opportunity of finding out that he had
arrived at years of discretion. Without any of its
obsessions or scruples he was taught the nature of
love in such a way that the memory of it accompanied him through life as a part of himself in relation to the powerful and healthy essence of nature.

" Aimée made an end of my virtue, and no doubt
the soil was a favourable one. On the homeward trip
we had several passengers, and among them a bounc-
ing Prussian woman. Properly speaking, it was now
the captain's turn to be smitten, and in fact he made
great play for her, but it was no good. She and I
had found a delightful nest in the sail-room, the door
of which opened on to the companionway. I filled
her up with a heap of the wildest yarns and assurances, and my Prussian, who was tremendously
thrilled, insisted on seeing me in Paris. I gave her
as my address: *La Farcy, rue Joubert.* This wasn't
nice of me and I had some qualms of conscience;
but I couldn't very well send her to my mother's. I
don't want to make myself out any worse or any
better than I am, but at eighteen there are germs
of all sorts of things in one."

Apart from this the life aboard the *Luzitano* was
to Paul mostly amusement which gave him an opportunity of developing his physical strength. He
was free and enjoyed his freedom. His existence
was an affair of the passing day; he thought little of

the future, had no dreams of great aims, scarcely felt that he had a call. He simply grew, developing into a well-built, powerful, and active young man. It took time, he did not shoot up suddenly; only at twenty was he fully grown. He had no special interests nor any ambitions, not even as a sailor. He was vegetating almost, but he was smart and handy at his work, without attracting particular attention. At twenty he entered on his military service. His mother, who had now moved to Saint-Cloud, had a growing sense that the sea did not offer her son any future. She spoke to her good friend and neighbour Gustave Arosa and together they arrived at the conclusion that at the end of his military service Paul should try banking. A not unusual course for a young man who had no very sure sense of what he was destined for, and in this case all the more natural as Arosa's son-in-law Calzado was manager of the banking firm of Bertin in the rue Lafitte.

Aline Gauguin did not live to see her son safely disposed. The Franco-Prussian War had broken out and Paul was stationed in the Cattegat on board the cruiser *Dessaix,* which was patrolling there. The house she lived in at Saint-Cloud was set on fire in the bombardment, and soon after Aline Gauguin died. She had been able to marry her daughter to a rich merchant of Colombia, but her son's future was only vaguely outlined.

Apart from the family portraits and a few valu-

able pieces of furniture everything was lost in the fire, including all the family papers. Paul Gauguin was thus an orphan and, broadly speaking, homeless when he landed in the spring of 1871 after completing his military duties.

Physically he had grown into a powerful and healthy man, trained in bodily exercises. A good fencer and boxer and an excellent swimmer. He was well built, rather above the middle height, broad-shouldered, narrow in the hips. His hands and feet were small, but strong, with long fingers. The head was narrow, with a long neck and a low forehead, the nose large, with a pronounced curve, and the mouth remarkable for the distance between it and the nose, the narrow upper lip, and the powerful, rather protruding lower lip. The mouth was the dominant feature in the narrow lower face with its slightly receding chin. The pale green eyes, not very large, were deeply set under straight brows; the eyelids were heavy and a pronounced far-sightedness gave him in general a rather absent look.

He had little growth of beard, but his hair was strong, reddish, and dark. His complexion was a uniform cool brown, with a greenish tinge in the shadows.

In a purely physical sense his life at sea had matured him; his emotional life had become somewhat more robust, but intellectually he had not yet arrived at complete consciousness. In a way his in-

telligence was still asleep; no doubt a certain natural
resolution in him had been intensified by the five
years at sea, but it was not yet directed to any goal.
He was impatient, however. In reality a man of pronounced ambition and at the same time sure of himself, he now felt he must get on rapidly. The only
question was how. The prospects offered by a sailor's
life did not really tempt him. It was no loss to him to
bid farewell to the sea, so he listened attentively to
the proposals of his influential well-wisher Arosa
and accepted them, feeling that they gave him a
chance of living independently and perhaps led to
a future. Who could tell?

The experiences and knowledge he had hitherto
acquired were not exactly the most suited to his future work, but one does not worry about that when
one is only twenty-three, can face life with courage,
and is free from the restraint of family and friends
and the advice they offer, and not troubled by any
definite idea of a future calling.

In reality his consciousness was still dormant, and
with it many latent powers and forces waiting for
release; and now everything was well disposed for
expansion.

He was a welcome guest at the house of Gustave
Arosa, where he was able to extend his intellectual
horizon. His host was a man of literary and artistic
interests, who owned a considerable collection of
the works of contemporary artists. He occupied his

leisure with photogravure among other things and had executed good reproductions of Delacroix and Courbet. This gave him a peculiar insight into the technique of the various artists and enabled him to judge of art with something of an expert's eye. And nothing pleased him more than talking about it, especially to his young protégé, who showed an evident interest in these things and had a remarkable power of receiving and retaining an impression of what he saw.

CHAPTER 2

On the little Danish island of Læssö in the middle
of the Cattegat there was born on September 7th,
1850 a fine and healthy baby girl, who was chris-
tened Mette Sofie. Her father was Theodor Gad, the
local magistrate, and her mother's name was Emilie,
née Lund. Mette was their first child, and she
showed a strong likeness to her father, a big, powerful man of Nordic type with a strong and healthy
disposition and a good deal of common sense. He
carried out his official duties with authority tem-
pered by leniency, asserted his dignity gently, ami-
ably, and as a matter of course by virtue of his handsome presence, his good opinion of people in general,
and a natural geniality which was coupled with
great sociability and a ready wit. But he died of facial
erysipelas at the age of forty, while district judge at
Thisted.

His widow moved to Copenhagen and joined her
mother, who was living on her pension as the widow

of a lieutenant-colonel. This together with Emilie
Gad's pension made up the modest income on which
the family had to support themselves and bring up
the five children: Mette Sofie, two more daughters,
Ingeborg and Pauline, and the boys Theodor and
Aage.

If the financial position of the home was not
exactly brilliant, it did not in any way hinder the
free expansion of the lively disposition which the
members of this family possessed in a very high
degree. Emilie was a capable and practical housekeeper who understood the arts of cookery and of
conducting a house with propriety, and her mother,
the colonel's widow, was an uncommonly lively
old lady, free-spoken and rather given to broad jokes.
She was the daughter of a blacksmith named Paulsen
at Bröndshöj, who besides his forge kept a little
tavern in that village just outside the capital, where
young artists and poets, Herman Wessel among
them, used often to meet convivially. And blacksmith Paulsen was as famous for his bodily strength
as his two daughters were for their beauty. Pauline
had married first a noted miniature-painter named
Lund, by whom she had her daughter Emilie, and
afterwards Lieutenant-Colonel Paulsen. But neither
the quiet and much older miniature-painter nor the
distinguished and stylish army officer had succeeded
in putting a polish on the merry daughter of the
blacksmith. Many years of barrack life had rather

intensified her liking for primitive and high-spirited conduct and for the use of strong language and boldness in her choice of subjects. She had also brought with her a good deal of imperiousness and obstinacy from her army life, but she found in her daughter a worthy opponent. With a delicate sarcasm that was all her own Emilie could drive people into a corner when it suited her; coolly and without passion she asserted her opinion and almost always got her own way. But this very opposition between the two women was productive of movement and life and stimulated the children's already awakened sense of the differences in human character, even within a narrow family circle. All three daughters were fine-grown, pretty girls; the two younger in particular were remarkable for their beauty. Mette was rather too big and powerful, and her features were strongly marked, almost like a man's, and full of character. Like the boys, they were all talented, quick at learning, and endowed with unusually good memories.

The family occupied a spacious top floor in a prosperous-looking house in Nyhavnsgade, centrally situated, one may say, but with a free and open view over the harbour. It was marked by good bourgeois taste; the solid mahogany furniture characteristic of a Danish official's home expressed in its rather chilly impersonality the orderly calm which its occupants were destined to maintain.

As the girls grew up into lively and sociable young

women they attracted many young people to the house in Nyhavn, which became more and more a rendezvous of cheerful society, the masculine part of which belonged largely to the Danish Navy, spirited and good-looking young men who could enjoy grandmother Paulsen's freedom of speech. Kept in check by the satire of her daughter Emilie, she gave a lively and unconstrained, but still decorous tone to the conversation. But it was a rule of the house that all attention was paid to the old lady, who had kept her looks wonderfully and even at the age of eighty was always ready for a schottische with one of the young men. But in reality the cadets were taken up with Ingeborg and Pylle (Pauline). Mette was cooler, sharper and wittier in repartee, and she looked for more brains in a man than did her sisters, though they too were critical, but not nearly so exacting as Mette. For one thing, her nature was simpler and less complicated and her emotions less impulsive and more limited, and, for another, she was obliged, as the eldest and most ambitious of the sisters, to think of making her own living, and this brought her into contact with other people than those of their narrower circle. Nor had she perhaps quite so sure a feeling as her two exceptionally pretty sisters that she would be successful in the game called love. She had not a pronounced erotic nature, did not give it much thought; she was practical, with a craving for freedom and independence. The unfor-

tunate issue of an early love-affair with a young naval officer perhaps made her force herself to think less of such things than she would otherwise have done. She was also rather short-spoken and quick to adopt a point of view; in many ways she matured early, as though she had skipped the enthusiasms of girlish years.

At seventeen she was appointed governess to the children of Estrup, the Prime Minister. It was a great change for her to come from a modest bourgeois home, in which two women asserted their authority, each in her own way, to a great country house where one man alone ruled absolutely. This was the most eminent man in Denmark, and it was not only in the King's Council that his will was law; it was the same on his estate and in his home; he was the man who saw everything, had an eye for every detail, and took care that all was done as he wished it. A tyrant in his way, but capable, open to new ideas, and in the main unselfish in all that he undertook. But he loved power; early and late his rule could be felt. He was staunchly conservative and loyal, an upholder of the privileges of the nobility, but he was entirely without snobbery and judged his fellow men by their capability rather than by the position they chanced to occupy in society. And his wife was an amiable woman, extremely musical, with a wonderful voice. To her husband she was entirely submissive, in spite of all the blue blood in

her veins, which was absent in his. But she admired and loved him. For that matter, she saw only the good side in everyone and was herself good and well-bred. Here Mette Gad became governess to five children, three boys and two girls. She not only was their governess, but soon became their confidential friend and was treated by their mother as one of the family. And His Excellency himself very soon took a fancy to her for her frank, straightforward manner and for her courage and presence of mind.

While with the Estrups, either on their great estate of Skaffögaard or in Copenhagen, when occasionally the whole family visited the capital during parliamentary sessions, the young woman met many leading men, and it amused the Prime Minister to introduce his guests to his governess and watch the intrepidity with which she conversed with them, urging the liberal views she brought from her home upon some dumbfounded ultra-conservative member of the government. Not that she was particularly fanatical in her point of view, but she had been brought up to look upon politics, religion, and morals as things which were capable of being discussed from various angles. It was nevertheless instructive for her to find herself in entirely different surroundings, where opinions were determined by very definite social points of view and political considerations. Among these people life was vastly more complicated and hemmed in by qualifications than it was in

the Gad family, where life was taken as a matter of course which arranged itself, provided one was physically well-favoured and reasonably cultured. All independent thought and action was confined within a framework which, even if it was wide enough to allow for liberal ideas, nevertheless had its bounds, which were very carefully observed by the family tradition. And the prevailing tone was admirably adapted to the exigencies of the time, without being either too reactionary or too liberal.

The favoured position Mette occupied in the Estrup household gave her ample opportunity of extending her knowledge, and with her quick brain, backed by an excellent memory, she had acquired such training in languages, especially French, that by the time she was twenty she began to think of foreign travel. But a couple of years were to go by before the chance came; difficult years for a girl who had outgrown her home. There had never been any great cordiality between her and her mother. As the eldest child she had been particularly attached to her father, who was her ideal before all others. Her real object now was to liberate herself and to be in a position to stand on her own feet.

It was a friend of her own age, Marie Heegaard, daughter of a rich manufacturer, who gave her this first chance. Heegaard wished his daughter to see something of the world — in other words, to go to Paris — and his confidence in Mette's sound sense

and linguistic attainments made him choose her as travelling companion for his daughter. Well supplied with money these two blonde daughters of the North set out for Paris, as independent young ladies, in the spring of 1873. The route they took was via Esbjerg and Rouen by a Danish steamer, whose chief engineer was a relative of Mette's. With him as a guide they travelled on to Paris and were deposited with Père Aubé, a sculptor, whose wife kept a very good pension where a few young Parisians without homes of their own were in the habit of taking their meals. Not infrequently they spent their evenings with their pleasant host and hostess and the foreign visitors, who in this way were brought in contact with the French spirit. And thus they made the acquaintance of educated Parisians who could guide them safely through the teeming life of the capital and familiarize them with the nature of the French language. Everything was thus favourably disposed for the two young Danish women's stay in Paris.

CHAPTER 3

IN everything except his relations with women Paul Gauguin was a pronounced optimist, with confidence in life, in other men, and, above all, in himself. Emancipated from conventions and dogmas, he trusted mainly to the faculty of combination which he felt he possessed to help him in his new position. He did not trouble himself to make inquiries and seldom explained his intentions. He abounded in initiative and usually acted after mature consideration, though he often obeyed an instinct which told him he must exert all his powers in order to achieve his end. But at the same time he was fully alive to anything that actively affected what he had in hand. Time after time this young and very impassive bank clerk surprised his older colleagues by the direct and decisive answers he returned to a question. All his notes were brief and concise, written in a small, clear, delicate hand. He kept his office hours like clockwork and always found something to occupy him.

It must be said that the rest of the bank's staff found this doubtless calm and polite but rather taciturn young man, who had lately exchanged the sailor's jumper for an office jacket, distinctly stand-offish. All their attempts to initiate him into the political, religious, and social interests which occupied them as average Parisians were in vain. After office hours, during which he was exclusively taken up with business, Paul Gauguin went his own way, usually to read at home; he did not feel much drawn to ordinary social intercourse and had no great talent for casual small talk. His constant occupation was with the values with which one has to deal in order to arrive at a positive understanding of life, and he found them above all in the poets. He chose particularly Balzac, Edgar Allan Poe, and Barbey d'Aurevilly. By way of lighter entertainment he visited the public dance halls on Saturdays, for he was fond of dancing and had a purely sexual impulse to attach himself to women without having to saddle himself with responsibilities of long duration. His childhood and youth had been passed almost entirely in the society of women and he had too often felt the spiritual pain of liberating oneself from their tender but powerful bonds. And this led him to prolonged reflection before surrendering himself to a love-affair.

Without any relations to whom he felt attached, without acquaintances that time had ripened into

friendship, Paul Gauguin was a rather lonely man. No one had any claim on him but himself. His ambition was to make something of his existence, though as yet he did not know what form it was to take. He could conceive no image of his future. All that was clear was that he was now given a chance and that he must avail himself of it to the best of his ability.

In the line of business he had adopted, the object was to make money by handling current financial values; nothing new was to be produced, the aim was to earn enough for one's requirements and to satisfy one's demands for the good things of life, to enjoy one's liberty and the independence which comes of earning enough to be able to buy things that are useful and bring one pleasure. The business as such interested him little and its methods had no attraction for him. He was no gambler, though he understood the game very well and always judged the financial situation calmly and deliberately, and with a never failing confidence in himself and his own opinion.

It was just this that Calzado was very quick to discover in his young assistant, and he was not content to watch Gauguin in silence, but encouraged him by constantly improving his position in the bank, so that at the end of two years he had every reason to consider himself a young man of good prospects.

He had no really extravagant habits, but liked to live well, in comfortable quarters, surrounded by pretty things, and was fond of good cooking. In fact,

he wanted to live comfortably without having to economize. But taking all his meals in a restaurant was not altogether to his liking. One was seldom allowed to eat in peace, unless one surrounded oneself with a wall of coldness. There was always somebody who addressed casual and irrelevant questions or perhaps entertained the whole restaurant with his political opinions, invariably ending with the customary appeal to his nearest neighbours for their absolute assent — an assent which, however annoying, was quite necessary if one desired peace. It was rather more agreeable at Père Aubé's pension, where there was a sense of home and the conversation generally turned on art and literature; but the whole thing was often rather casual and a well-bred young man was obliged to take a part on one side or the other if he did not wish to be regarded as a boor.

Paul Gauguin was inclined to envy his only real companion in the bank, Émile Schuffenecker, a good-natured fellow whose hobby was drawing and painting in his leisure time. He was a few years older than Gauguin, but admired the latter, looking up to him as a budding financial genius. He had just installed himself in a comfortable home, had collected a few pictures by good artists, and had a pretty and sensible wife, who never troubled her husband or her visitors with uncalled-for or superfluous explanations. On the contrary, Gauguin found her one of the few women with whom one could talk straight

out, without being either profound or involved. She
was tall too, with a face full of character. In reality
he thought a good deal more of her than of her husband, who was rather small and insignificant, somewhat vacillating in his infinite amiability and not
very settled in his opinions. And yet one had no impression that she was the ruling spirit. On the contrary, the relations between them were harmonious,
such as exist between two people who respect each
other's personal freedom. On her side Madame
Schuffenecker felt a decided sympathy for her husband's rather taciturn and very self-sufficient friend.
As a natural, sensible, and unprejudiced woman she
perceived that the arrogance of his manner concealed
a powerful and manly instinct with very violent feelings, to which a remarkable intelligence denied an
outlet.

Actually there was no financial reason to prevent
Gauguin from settling down in a home like that of
his friend, and the possibility began to hover before
him. But he had not yet come across any woman in
Paris whose looks and character gave him sufficient
confidence to make the experiment.

Chance was to decide, as it had so often done before in his life and hitherto without his having any
ground for complaint.

One fine day in spring Gauguin on leaving his
office paused for a moment at the corner of the
boulevard des Italiens, hesitating where to dine. The

horse-chestnuts were flowering; their bright sprigs
of bloom swayed in the mild spring breeze among
the masses of green foliage which were outlined
against the tall shining walls on the other side of the
boulevard. A young brightly dressed woman brushed
against the overcoat he carried over his arm. He gave
a start and turned hesitatingly, following with his
eyes the motions of her body as she walked on. But
then he took the opposite direction towards the place
de l'Opéra, still rather uncertain where he was going. He did not feel inclined to go to the restaurant
in the place de la Bourse, which he generally frequented, or to the little brasserie on the corner in the
quarter where he lodged. Perhaps he would go to
Père Aubé's, where he hadn't been for ever so long,
or to some new place farther out in Montparnasse.
He turned down the avenue de l'Opéra, which lay
before him broad and bright in the spring sunshine,
and followed the stream of business people who were
on their way home to the left bank of the Seine. He
could still put off making up his mind till he reached
the neighbourhood of the pension. But, after all, it
would be pleasant to meet people one could talk to.
He was in the vein for that and rather dreaded having to sit and mope by himself all the evening. And
finally he decided to go up to Aubé's.

In the dining-room Madame sat talking to two
fair-haired young women. One in particular attracted his attention. She did most of the talking, not

very fluently and with a pronounced foreign accent. He noticed her voice; it was powerful, with a slight roughness, almost like a man's; but it was not harsh, rather broad, with an open ring, and she spoke calmly and restrainedly, pronouncing the words clearly. He was introduced: Mette Gad. She was tall, broad-chested, simply and naturally built, with large, frank features in a face of unusual strength. She was fair-haired, without any decided colouring of either hair or complexion.

What attracted him was her healthy freshness, the harmony and simplicity of her presence. Even the slightly foreign note appeared natural and set off her personality.

In the course of the evening's conversation, about things great and small, he soon found out that she shared many of his interests and that her view of most things was based on independent conclusions which often surprised him by their maturity and open-mindedness. There was something fresh and springlike about her which suited the mood he had been in all day. He suddenly remembered the light brush of a woman's arm on the boulevard and looked at the young woman before him, following with his eyes the movement of her body. Then he got up to say good-night, promised Madame Aubé, as usual, to come again soon, expressing the hope that he would meet the young ladies, and as he repeated all the customary phrases there was perhaps an un-

wonted genuineness in his tone. He felt there was something behind his words.

The days passed quickly that spring; before he was aware of it the pavement struck warm as he went down the avenue de l'Opéra in the afternoon on his way to the Aubés'. The intervals between his meetings with the two young Danish ladies grew shorter and shorter; soon there was no interval at all.

They knew where he was in the habit of lunching and liked the distinctly masculine tavern opposite the Bourse, which now seemed to him cosier and more homelike than before. He was a little surprised at the familiar way in which they dropped in on him there and parted from him when he went back to his office. It was something new to him as a Frenchman, this free and easy tone, so natural and unforced that it must be in their blood. And he liked it.

The intercourse between the three young people was soon marked by a natural intimacy to which Gauguin had been little accustomed hitherto. His manner became easier, less reserved, and more communicative. And by degrees their conversation acquired a freely confidential tone, as when Mette Gad with a racy humour all her own expressed her annoyance with the impertinences to which her luxuriant figure often exposed her from male admirers.

To tell the truth, this same healthy shapeliness had proved very attractive to Gauguin, and the more he got to know her, the stronger was the impression

it made on his susceptible senses. At the same time he
had discovered a quality about her which gave one
to understand that she was an independent personality and more inclined to be guided by her clear and
sound intelligence than by her emotions. Her interest
in erotic matters was a cool one and largely con-
trolled by her practical sense and her humour. But
that in itself reassured him and enabled him to overcome much of the excessive deference and reserve
which he had been accustomed in his youth to ob-
serve towards women of his own class. A deference
at which he often chafed and which hindered his
natural self-expression.

Imperceptibly the talks between him and Mette
Gad became more intimate and with this growing
intimacy they talked more and more about themselves, leading up to the question which called for
a decision, and as they both knew their own minds
the answer was not long in doubt. In the course of
the summer they agreed to be married as soon as
possible.

At her home in Denmark Mette's decision caused
no anxiety. From her own calm and rational letters
and what they heard from Marie Heegaard on her
return, the family concluded that Mette's future
husband was a responsible young man in a good position. The only person whose advice Paul Gauguin
was bound in duty to ask, Gustave Arosa, took an
immediate fancy to the young woman his protégé

had chosen and was pleased that the latter had come to a decision which could only encourage him to build up a safe and solid future for himself.

A little apartment was found and on November 22nd, 1873 they were married in the Lutheran church of the rue Chauchat. Religion meant nothing either to him or to her, but as Gauguin did not belong to any church it was decided out of consideration for certain members of the Gad family to supplement the obligatory civil marriage by a religious ceremony.

Before many months had passed Gauguin felt sure that he had no reason to regret his choice. In fact he was astonished at the ease with which his wife was able to accommodate herself to the foreign surroundings in which she found herself. She now spoke French fluently and she was a great talker, giving him a gay and witty account of her doings during the day and of the people she had met. In short, she lived her own life while he was at business and never troubled him with unnecessary questions, very seldom wearied him with repetitions, being keenly alive to all that happened at the moment and having a wide range of interests, especially for what was actual. Rather rapid and superficial in her judgments, perhaps more occupied with the meaning of a thing than with its execution, but always prompted by sound sense. Actually it only amused him, being himself rather stolid in his thoroughness, to watch

the ease and self-possession with which this young woman behaved in company and in most of the affairs of life. Though not lacking in character or individuality, she was uncommonly sociable, and he liked that. He knew very well that he was not socially gifted and was glad to see that this did not in any way hamper her free expansion. They respected each other's health and strong vitality. And the fine and lusty boy she bore him in October 1874 increased and strengthened this feeling. He was proud to be a father and did not keep it to himself, confiding amongst others in Marie Heegaard's mother.

" Mette would have been so happy to show you her baby. Let me tell you he's a fine child; it is not only our father's and mother's hearts that say so; everyone says the same. White as a swan and strong as Hercules. I'm not quite sure if he is amiable; very likely not, with so cross-grained a father."

Some months before the birth of Émile, Gauguin had begun to draw, and Mette was rather surprised to see how well he got on, for he had never before shown signs of any ability in that direction. Though she knew from her visits to Arosa and to Schuffenecker that he was interested in painting and often went to exhibitions, there was nothing in the way he talked about it to disclose that he himself had ever tried his hand. And now he drew hands and feet and now and then herself as she sat resting. And

METTE GAUGUIN
1879

GAUGUIN'S SON EMILE
1875

he always went to work with his usual thoroughness, studying the object very carefully and drawing the same hand over and over again in the most various positions. After Émile's birth her husband was more and more taken up by his drawing and began to paint as well; she herself had enough to do with her baby and was only pleased when on Sundays he set out with his paint-box for the environs of Paris or accompanied Schuffenecker on an occasional evening to the Académie Colarassi to make sketches.

To Gauguin himself this was an enjoyable relaxation for his leisure hours, a kind of intellectual sport which fascinated and tranquillized him after the dry, mechanical work of the day, the noting of prices and investments which had a stimulating, but at the same time a blunting effect on him, since according to his idea all this work only produced negative values. But it also tickled his vanity and in a way spurred his desire of self-assertion, when his drawings and paintings gave a result satisfactory to his eye. Actually he had no conscious artistic aim. His colour sense was uncertain and approached that of the Fontainebleau school, and his drawing was conventional, with a very careful study of the model. It was the purely manual element that occupied him. For this reason his visits to exhibitions became more frequent and he now had a more observant eye for technical niceties. At the Colarassi he joined " *les fauves*," the wild beasts who scorned the corrections

of a teacher, and here he listened to the budding artists' discussions for and against the elect of the Salon. Most of them, like Schuffenecker, sided with the Impressionists, who in '72 had held their first exhibition at Nadar's. He had noticed their work, especially that of Renoir, but they had no very great attraction for him. He was more occupied with form, simple and perfect. He admired an artist like Millet. The big, powerful women that painter drew appealed to his eye, and the primitive strength, the vigorous, naked luxuriance of life and nature in Millet's art had more to say to his mind and senses than the beauty of the momentary vision.

But the more Gauguin worked with his material and discovered all the difficulties involved, the greater was its fascination for him, and for the fun of the thing he sent in a picture for the Salon of '76 and got it accepted. A landscape, careful and elaborate in its workmanship, the prevailing tones of which were dark green and grey. A new name in the Salon, but no new note that was capable of attracting attention. Nor did he himself attach much importance to his " debut " as an artist. Neither his friend Schuffenecker nor his wife knew anything about it.

For that matter, his work at the bank gave him enough to think about. Calzado had entrusted him with the important and responsible task of closing the day's current business on the Bourse, and, con-

—*44*—

fiding in his calm judgment and wishing to encourage him, had given him a free hand to an extent which enabled Gauguin to do business on his own account. Although, to begin with, his profits did not amount to much — as usual he went to work calmly and systematically — they were sufficient to let him turn his thoughts to a more commodious home. This became all the more necessary as on Christmas Eve 1876 his wife presented him with a daughter, who was named after his mother.

In the spring they moved into a new apartment, No. 79 rue des Fourneaux, in a house owned by the well-known marble-cutter Paul Bouillot, who had his workshop across the yard. Here Gauguin had opportunities of seeing how a work of sculpture was transferred to stone and it interested him to such an extent that he himself took to modelling — a bust of his wife which Bouillot carved in marble, with himself as a pupil. And as the next step he himself under Bouillot's direction cut the bust he had modelled of his son Émile. With growing astonishment the skilful craftsman witnessed the young stockbroker's dexterity and sure eye for form, and the work helped Gauguin himself to develop his sense for material and for form, which plays a far more important part in sculpture than in painting, where so many other factors contribute to give effective expression to the eye's conception of reality.

Nevertheless it was the material that attracted

him most. Even if its decorative possibilities were not yet quite clear to him, it delighted him to surround himself with beautiful things; he liked to arrange his home, to choose its colours; he would even take to embroidery on occasion and showed a fondness for vivid colours. He bought oriental carpets and earthenware, particularly Rouen faience with its richly coloured decoration. His taste was not marked by any definite sense of style, but all the things with which he surrounded himself showed quality and decorative pictorial feeling, and anything like symmetry was almost tabooed.

All this bore witness to Gauguin's domesticity, and in her own way Mette was equally fond of her home; but she had far more taste for society than he and saw how important it would be for him as a business man to extend his circle of acquaintance. But in this she had little or no support from him, so that the company they entertained consisted mainly of her women friends. He acted the polite host until the conversation was well started, but seized the first opportunity of vanishing quietly. And she had grown so used to his doing exactly what suited him that she was neither surprised nor annoyed when one evening, after having been absent a good while, he came back in his nightshirt and begged the ladies not to let him interrupt them, he had only come to get a book. His manner was so calm and so natural that nobody felt any awkwardness in continuing the con-

versation, which had scarcely been disturbed by this unusual, but actually rather amusing interlude.

As a matter of fact, the sense of independence which Gauguin asserted so strongly suited her quite well. With her emphatically active nature she had enough to occupy her, and he very seldom troubled her with any requests which limited her freedom of movement. She may have thought a little more appreciation of her initiative was due to her; but she was bound to acknowledge on her side that she took no interest at all in what obviously concerned him most, though she made up for it by the pride and admiration she showed for his capability and accuracy in business and was appreciative of his generosity in all money matters. She herself was not close-fisted, but life had taught her the necessity of a certain degree of economy and carefulness. Paul on the other hand had an almost unlimited confidence in his power of finding money. On this as on most other points he was an incorrigible optimist, but at the same time he worked like a horse. She might often silently thank providence that he had no exaggerated craving for luxuries. The only thing was a certain weakness for narcotics, such as tobacco and brandy, without their having any apparent effect on him.

Mette had no cause for complaint, nor did she complain. Her letters home were as contented as they were matter-of-fact. Paul works hard and

makes money; even in his leisure he has to occupy himself with something, and at present he is generally busy with painting and drawing. Both the children are well. Émile rather fidgety and troublesome, but Aline quiet and thoughtful like her father. She herself is fit and well. Rather sorry that she is going to have another child. — Such, more or less, was the tenor of most of her letters; rarely if ever did they contain a hint of homesickness.

In May 1879 Clovis was born, a fine big baby like the others, but fair.

Even after the acceptance of his picture by the Salon, Gauguin had no claim to call himself an artist, but his eyes were becoming more and more open to the fact that the progress he was making in his painting had a greater positive value for him than was offered by his business. His works did not yet satisfy his personal ambition, but they opened up a prospect of something which occupied his consciousness in a far higher degree than the almost mechanical game of the Bourse. It did not occur to him outside business hours to look up people who might give him useful information for his stock-exchange operations. On the other hand he called on art dealers and through them met artists who, very differently from his colleagues in the bank, gave him the assurance that there are values one can neither buy nor sell.

The artists he met in this way were very young

LANDSCAPE
1876

PHOTO, O. VÆRING, OSLO

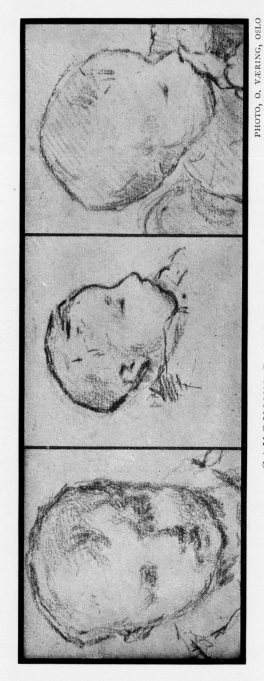

GAUGUIN'S DAUGHTER ALINE

1877

men, all more or less taken up with new ideas about painting and by the stir they were making, not only in artistic circles, but also among a certain section of the public. The agitation ran high around the Impressionists in particular, a group of young painters who as yet had no definite program, but who by holding exhibitions of their own were beginning to assert themselves in the face of the official Salon, where the leading men in their hidebound interpretation of classical ideals did what they could to exclude everything which might be suspected of aiming at other æsthetic values than those prescribed by the worthy representatives of official art in the French Republic. In fact they even looked with distrust on all art which reflected the enjoyment of life so splendidly expressed by French painters before the great Revolution. It not only offended their republican views but often gave them a feeling that revolutionary opinions opposed to the French Republic were about to assert themselves. Art had become a vehicle of propaganda for moral and political opinions and had degenerated into a conception of style to which the official academy had given its approval as art. But it was a conception of style which had nothing to do with the healthy life of the French citizen, and when that life was depicted it was quite likely to raise a scandal. A guard had to be posted by Manet's *Olympia* to prevent its being damaged by a public which was scandalized because the nude

model was a pretty girl of the people with a simple black velvet ribbon round her throat, and not as she ought to have been, a courtesan fresh from the hairdresser.

At the beginning of the seventies the Impressionists were no esoteric circle that had formed about a common artistic aim, but it chanced that just in those years a number of sound, vigorous, and independent talents came to maturity, to whom nature and life had more to say than had the approved interpretation thereof. They needed light, air, and natural life in order to expand; and they all felt that the atmosphere of the official Salon did not supply this need. But it was the road which led by way of critics and art dealers to the public. A new road must therefore be opened up, but where? Perhaps through Nadar in the boulevard des Capucines, who speculated in novelties and had already found room for such curiosities as Renoir, Monet, and Pissarro. Or through Durand-Ruel in the rue le Peletier, who had resolutely backed Édouard Manet, the most discussed artist in Paris at that time, for years refused or demonstratively mishung at the Salon, abused by the critics of the leading newspapers, and often pilloried there for the benefit of the art-loving public which was easily scandalized; defended by powerful but dangerous pens like Zola and Baudelaire, and admired by those contemporary artists who could see a future for French art. He himself would only ac-

knowledge the Salon as his forum, in spite of the
terrible fits of despondency to which its ill-treatment
year by year subjected his sensitive and lofty spirit.
Well might his friend Baudelaire write to Champ-
fleury: " Manet has a forceful talent, a talent which
will carry him on, but he has a weak character. He
seems stupefied and reduced to despair by the shock.
What also strikes me is the joy of the blockheads,
who believe him to be lost."

Baudelaire was actually rather alarmed about
Manet's state of mind, which made him write to a
woman friend of himself and Manet:

" When you see Manet tell him this from me —
that all kinds of opposition, scorn, insults, injustice,
are excellent things, and that he is an ungrateful person if he does not thank them. I know very well that
he will find a certain difficulty in understanding my
theory. Painters always desire immediate success.
The truth is that Manet's gifts are so splendid and
so easy to work with that he is bound to be miserable
if he loses courage. He will never be able entirely to
bridge over the gaps in his temperament. But he has
a temperament, that is the main thing, and he does
not seem to see that the greater the injustice, the better will be his position — so long as he does not lose
his head. I am sure you will be able to say all this to
him in a light-hearted way, so as not to wound him."

But although Manet was extremely sensitive he
never turned bitter or bore a grudge against anyone,

and he never lost courage for long. Right up to the time of his too early death in 1883 he sent his pictures almost yearly to the Salon and it was only in the two last years that they received the treatment to which they were entitled.

Thus he always declined to send anything to other collective exhibitions, even when the Impressionists decided to hold their first exhibition at Nadar's in the boulevard des Capucines.

It was this exhibition, by the way, which gave them their name, and this was due to a picture by Claude Monet called *L'Impression*, which was ridiculed by the critics as " indeed nothing but an impression. And for that matter the same might be said of most of the pictures exhibited." The tone adopted by official criticism, led by Albert Wolff, the dreaded art critic of the *Figaro*, a blend of violent indignation and ridicule, piqued the curiosity of the public and brought crowds to the exhibition. Contact had now been established with the public; although, to begin with, their attitude was not friendly, at any rate people did not pass by indifferently. Attention had been aroused, and this would lead to understanding. And in the following years the Impressionists held exhibitions at various places, Durand-Ruel's among others, until at the end of the seventies the Salon des Indépendants was instituted, where anyone could exhibit without being passed by a hanging committee. This exhibition, which a few

years later became a permanent institution, had the
support of the most notable of those artists who had
previously arranged the exhibition at Nadar's.

As has been said above, the Impressionists could
not be described as a group with any definite program, nor had they in a strict sense anyone who could
be called a leader. The most significant among them,
such as Renoir, Cézanne, and Degas, had neither the
personal qualities nor the desire to gather a following
about them. Renoir was too simple and modest,
Cézanne too little interested in other men's work,
and Degas too solitary and retiring by nature. If he
took part in these exhibitions it was chiefly out of
sympathy with and interest in the efforts of younger
artists, and because these, in addition to their admiration for him as an artist, had an immense respect
for his unusually open-minded and authoritative
judgment of art in general. His view of it was not
determined by the question whether the thing was
beautiful, but by its character and harmony, with a
very strong sense for and a keen perception of the
distinguishing marks of technique, and, above all, of
the characteristic movements and balance of the
human body in every natural function. For these
reasons he quarrelled with the official art of the Salon.
Not only that, but he had gradually acquired a profound distrust of its leaders and their motives. He
belonged to a very influential and wealthy family
and thus was well acquainted with the circles who

took part in the annual function of the opening of the Salon. He had soon observed that the considerations on which the choice of works was based had little to do with art and were often scarcely compatible with its nature and checked any free and independent development of art. His strong self-dependence soon disgusted him with all this cliquishness; the fashionable drawing-rooms of the day were no places for him. All his interests were bound up with his art. When he appeared in the pulsating life of Paris it was only for the sake of observing it; he led as a rule a very retired life, and as he was financially independent publicity was not necessary to him as to so many other artists. This again made him sympathetic to the efforts younger artists were making to arrive at a personal form. He interested himself in their work and was willing to support their efforts to find a public; but his participation in their exhibitions did not mean much more than this.

More than any other, Camille Pissarro was the driving power of the movement. He was the oldest of them, born in 1830 in the Danish West Indies. His father was of Portuguese-Jewish descent, French-born, and his mother was a Creole. Camille Pissarro had received a commercial education, but had given up business at the age of twenty-five in order to become a painter. Properly speaking he had had no teacher, nor had he attended any studio. His talent was neither particularly rich nor individual,

but he was a gifted, intelligent man with a very delicate artistic instinct. Apart from seven years' schooling in Paris he had spent his whole childhood and youth in the West Indies, and before he made up his mind to be a painter he had travelled a good deal in South America. His vision had thus been developed by a great variety of foreign influences. And as he was no ordinary observer, but on the contrary a very accurate inquirer, he had arrived even as a young man at a very personal way of looking at things which did not come to rest when confronted with the artistic prototypes he found in Paris. His whole development therefore is marked by a continual quest. At first he admired Corot most of all. Corot's vigorous and healthy worship of nature and the brilliance of his colouring gave him a wealth of inspiration, but the artless, almost religiously simple relation between this master and his motive was foreign to Pissarro's inquiring and decidedly theoretical nature. It found no favourable soil in a mind and an artistic talent which had first to be cultivated by the intellect. Intellect he had, and he knew how to use his eyes with an uncommon insight into artistic values, coupled with a special capacity for investigating the technical possibilities of the material. A cool flame burned in his soul, and after prolonged search and many changes in his point of view he produced works of great value, inspired by a vigorous and healthy delight in nature and a rich and brilliant

use of colour. This was due in great measure to the younger painters whose leader he became, in a way, under the name of the Impressionists. He for his part was useful to them through his clear and intelligent criticism and through interpreting to them things which they had not yet thoroughly sifted. While many of those who had founded the school, and among them the most significant, deserted or, like Renoir and Cézanne, entirely renounced it, Pissarro continued to uphold Impressionism and laid down its artistic program. He thus acquired a very considerable influence over the young painters who entered the world of art in the midst of the conflicts that announced the modern movement, not only in France, but all over Europe.

The artists whom Paul Gauguin met at first were not among the most important and their notions of the still rather vague idea of Impressionism as a form whose special object was to seize the flying moment did not appear immediately obvious and afforded him no satisfactory solution of the very important problems with which Manet, Degas, and Renoir were struggling, artists who appealed more and more to his attention. Without its being clear to himself, it was the very nature of art that now absorbed him.

What previously was only an occupation for his leisure hours now became a subject for reflection which engaged him continually, in spite of the increasing success of his business on the Bourse, which

GAUGUIN'S WIFE
1879

GAUGUIN'S WIFE
1880

enabled him without diffidence to rent a little house in the rue Carcel. The house, which belonged to the painter Jobbé-Duval, had a little garden attached to it, surrounded by a high wall, and a studio where he could work in peace at his paintings on holidays and in the evenings. In the rue Carcel their third child, Clovis, was born and Mette had her hands full with looking after the house and the children. She was happy and contented; Paul's painting mania, as she called it, disturbed her as little as it interested her. Paul attended to his business, made money, spared no expense to make his home pretty and comfortable, and, now that he had provided himself with a work-room, was nearly always at home. Though perhaps Mette might have wished herself a more sociable and entertaining husband, she appreciated his chivalry, the care he took for the welfare of herself and the children, and the esteem with which he obviously regarded her own good humour. Her abundance of this quality and her sense of comedy would often make her slightly vexed with the solemn way in which he took everything and with the impossibility of ever making him laugh. But on the other hand he would astonish her with his clear, sound judgment of people and affairs and with the downright way in which he expressed his opinion without showing any surprise if she or others differed from it. Mette was content. Even if Paul was heavy, he was not difficult and never laid any re-

straint on her freedom of action, which to her was one of the most essential good things of life.

Nor did Gauguin complain of his life; his ample income gave him full opportunity of pursuing his interests, even though the bank took up rather much of his valuable time. To be sure, he encountered ever increasing difficulties in his painting. The criticism he directed against the painters with whom he mixed recoiled very often on himself and gave him no more encouragement than did the admiration of his friend Schuffenecker. He often felt himself to be what most of the others regarded him, the banker's clerk, whose pictures appeared astonishing, considering his position, but were not to be taken too seriously. Mette's jocular allusions to his *idée fixe* were not always passed over in silence, but his desire to penetrate to the root of the matter continued, growing more urgent day by day.

One day chance threw him together with Camille Pissarro. And Gauguin interested Pissarro. He himself had been in business and there was something in Gauguin's character and personality which told him that the exotic and somewhat unusual elements in the young Parisian banker had points of contact with similar features in himself. This not merely interested him, it aroused his sympathy; and the feeling was mutual. When Pissarro spoke about art in his thorough, rather dogmatic way, Gauguin listened attentively and understood his theories far better

than the painters' jargon he had been accustomed to hear. It was not merely the other's personality that attracted him; he felt that all his own endeavours to arrive at clarity concerning the nature of painting might find an excellent support in the realism with which Pissarro treated the subject and in the very thorough study this artist, who was nearing fifty, had devoted to painting before he himself had arrived at a form which satisfied him.

Gauguin invited Pissarro to visit him, and from that time the leading thread in Gauguin's life began to be spun in earnest. Mette had no presentiment that this man was destined to exert a fateful influence over her husband; she was only glad that at last he should bring a visitor to the house. She liked Pissarro and he soon came to enjoy her society, so it was not long before he was a constant guest at the rue Carcel. He and she quickly discovered that they were in a way compatriots, and even if this circumstance in itself did not mean very much it provided a certain bond of union which facilitated the transition from polite conversation to natural companionship. Mette had confidence in this man who obviously had a good influence on Paul's spirits, which during the last year had frequently been somewhat depressing. She was quite aware that he stimulated her husband's painting hobby, but even he did not seem to take it too seriously. Pissarro, however, thought there was nothing better or more wholesome than that a business

man should follow in his leisure time an interest which gave a meaning to his existence. Her husband had talent and if led in the right direction it would enhance his obvious interest in art and strengthen his already very lively sense of its real values. At the same time art had a financial value. If one bought with intelligence and understanding one might be laying up a capital which would go on increasing, while at the same time one's walls would give pleasure and intellectual cultivation. Pissarro was convinced that works by the young men who were now championing new ideas would increase considerably in value. One might buy pictures by Manet, Renoir, and Cézanne at prices which in twenty years' time would have risen tenfold. To a smart man of business an interest in art was only a stimulant, which enhanced his sense of the real value of money as instrumental in useful production. As a commodity money was valueless, it merely passed from one pocket to another. With this Gauguin entirely agreed, as did his wife in a way, only she thought there were more useful things than pictures. As the daughter of an official she had not much grasp of capital-appreciation. She judged future prospects from the point of view of increased or diminished income. That a painting or a piece of furniture might cost a cabinet minister's salary astonished her beyond measure. She found it altogether unreasonable and absurd.

That Paul, instead of playing billiards and spending his money at the café sat at home messing about with a paint-brush for his own amusement was really an excellent thing. His income had now reached a far higher figure than she had ever dreamed of. No doubt it did give her something of a shock when her husband got their nurse Justine, a strong, good-looking woman with black hair and a white skin, to sit to him in the nude. But Justine told her mistress that that was nothing out of the way — why, she had sat to Delacroix himself, so Madame need not worry.

Pissarro was a theorist and at the same time a practical man. To him art was not only a manifestation of talent and inspiration, it was just as much a handicraft of very high value, to the technique of which he had devoted an ardent study. As a landscape-painter he had occupied himself specially with the light-effects of colour and had endeavoured assiduously to achieve these effects without having to impair the intrinsic value of the primary colours. He was not the first to make practical use in painting of the fact that the very source of light, the light of the sun, is split up by the spectrum into the primary colours, but he was one of the first who tried to carry it out consistently, and perhaps he was the most zealous preacher of the gospel of the primary colours. Nothing could have been better for Gauguin. Quite unconsciously he had always felt the attraction of

strong and pure colour, but he had never succeeded in achieving it in his painting. Now Pissarro put him on the right road, and even if the older man had no exaggerated idea of Gauguin's talent, he had to acknowledge that his pupil showed an uncommon aptitude in setting his palette with pure and strong colours and in using them with a boldness and a sense of vigorous and harmonious combinations which were surprising. But Gauguin seemed disinclined to adopt the actual principle of arranging the primary colours in a definite order so that together they formed a unity which evoked the idea of light, reflection, and shade; whereas he endeavoured to combine a plastic feeling with a decorative colour harmony. And Pissarro with his strict and consistent upholding of purely pictorial principles considered this altogether too aimless. He was inclined to look upon his pupil as an amateur with a highly developed sense of artistic values and a gift for expressing this sense, now in painting, now in purely decorative schemes, and now in sculpture, both clay-modelling and wood-carving.

Everything this man laid his hands on had to be shaped in some way or other, but without any definite line, and evidently with no other object than satisfying his personal taste.

Gauguin never let it be known that Pissarro had found him the means of overcoming many of the obstacles he had previously had to contend with. He

grappled with greater problems, especially figure subjects, which had always been his chief interest. Mette was reluctantly pressed into the service, now in her evening dress with the pink bodice, low neck, and short sleeves, which showed off her full figure, now in a comfortable everyday frock, busy with her needlework. She found it consumedly boring, but was nevertheless rather flattered and reassured by his intense occupation with her luxuriant charms, and she noticed also that it increased the intimacy of their relations if she thus participated in what was his chief interest. At the same time she felt instinctively that it would not do to let Justine be the only one to foster this. When she saw him at his easel she had an inkling of the turmoil that was seething in her husband's mind. And thank goodness she had not sat to Delacroix himself.

In reality Gauguin was leading a double life and beginning to play for high stakes in both of them. With decided success as far as the Bourse was concerned. In one year he made forty thousand francs, so he had no hesitation in satisfying the desire he had long felt of buying pictures. He spent fifteen thousand francs at a stroke. And guided by his own expert eye, aided by Pissarro's advice and good connections, he bought well and cheaply, so that he acquired at once an excellent collection of pictures by Manet, Renoir, Degas, Sisley, Cézanne, Pissarro and Guillaumin. The two last-named he knew very well per-

sonally. Pissarro had brought Guillaumin to visit him, but the pictures he valued most were Cézanne's, in spite of their detesting each other. Pissarro, who was a very good friend of Cézanne, had several times tried to bring them together, and the Cézannes did not live far from the rue Carcel. But Cézanne entertained a very decided distrust of everything that smacked of the bourgeois; he could not stand Manet, for instance, whose outward appearance was that of the elegant boulevardier. Gauguin was to him merely the well-dressed banker, and besides that he was by no means unassuming in his criticism of art and literature. Thus he failed to realize the importance of Zola. In his opinion this author's novels were concerned far too much with people's digestions, good or bad. And what language!

" In Émile Zola's books the washerwoman and the concierge both speak a French which I don't find inspiring. When they stop talking Zola continues without suspecting it in the same tone and the same kind of French."

An utterance like this annoyed Cézanne, who was a friend and admirer of Zola. For his part Gauguin looked upon the rude and somewhat unkempt Provençal, whose language was apt to be pretty coarse, as a boor whom it was best to keep at a distance. And Cézanne's complete indifference to money, with the irregularities in money matters that resulted from it, was not to his liking. He himself had always been

very strict in these matters, and it made him extremely unhappy to find himself momentarily in a
position where he could not pay his way. Indeed, he
carried his dislike so far as to forbid his six-year-old
son Émile to play with Cézanne's son Paul, who was
a little older. But he admired the painter Cézanne to
the extent of copying one of his pictures. He also
copied David's *Joseph and Potiphar's Wife.* The plasticity which these two painters had arrived at, each
in his own way, interested him in the highest degree,
but he still did not see how he was to combine this
with a vigorous and decorative colouring without
violating his sense of reality and his instinct for nature. Japanese woodcuts gave him a pointer. They
combine the decorative with a reality and to some
extent also with nature, but give no expression of
that delight in form which he admired in Ingres
and Millet, and have none of the purely sensuous
feeling for nature which is expressed so wonderfully
by these two peasant lads, though without the simple
and uncompounded feeling of form that Gauguin
had found in primitive art at the Musée Guimet,
which he visited so often to refresh his memories of
childhood and of his life at sea. And this gave rise
to vague longings for something widely separated
from his present position. Not in one way alone, but
in many ways he felt he was a square peg in a round
hole. His position in society as a business man did not
entitle him to entertain these longings, nor indeed

to regard himself seriously as an artist. And nobody else took him seriously as an artist. He himself often had doubts; his versatile gifts, his complicated nature continually involved him in artistic problems for the satisfactory solution of which he, as a European, a Frenchman, and a Parisian, possessed too few data, especially now that all contemporary art, which he admired in many ways, was so typically French.

As yet all his efforts led only to vague results; but even though he occasionally had to agree with his master Pissarro that his attempts were amateurish, the dream was taking shape within him, he had an idea of its outlines. His imagination had taken him captive; induced by his self-confidence and optimism, he made up his mind to exhibit at the Salon des Indépendants in 1880. His pictures, a number of landscapes, were received with the benevolence shown to a man who had made good progress, obviously due to the judicious guidance of Pissarro.

An attention which, broadly speaking, was not overwhelmingly encouraging. A chance meeting with Manet did something to restore his self-confidence. Manet spoke of his pictures with kindly appreciation, and not knowing quite how to take this praise from the much-admired master, Gauguin apologized for himself, saying he was a business man who only painted in his spare time. Only an amateur, in fact. " Oh," said Manet, " the only amateurs are those who paint bad pictures." A fairly innocent re-

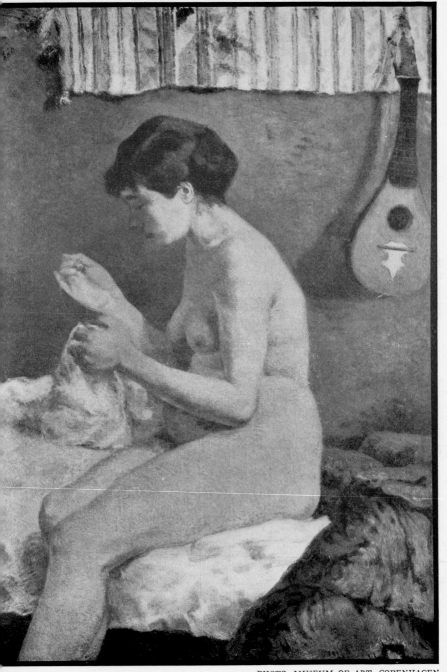

NUDE
1880

TWO SIDES OF WOODEN BOX CARVED WITH RELIEFS
OF BALLET-GIRLS AFTER DEGAS

1881

mark, but it went home. So he wasn't merely an amateur — a dilettante. That was just what he wanted to hear.

The following year was in many ways a decisive one in his career. If his self-confidence had faded somewhat into the background, his ambition had taken its place. He determined now to prove to himself and others that he was a painter, and he grappled with exacting problems, in which the figure was of paramount importance; among them a fairly large picture with Justine as his model, sitting naked on the side of a bed and mending her linen. And side by side with his painting he worked at wood-carving, among other things a little chest with reliefs after Degas's ballet-girls. In that year Degas had contributed to the exhibition a series of his pictures of the ballet, and Gauguin had been much struck by them. Here he found something of what he was seeking, the interplay of civilized scenes and primitive forces. A connection between decorative form and rhythmical movement from real life. Unvarnished truth and the primitive beauty of the human body are sharply outlined, inspired by a wonderful sensitiveness, behind the external and decorative mask with which Degas's models are nearly always provided.

When Gauguin chose Justine as his model it was in the first place because she belonged to the luxuriant type of womanhood he liked and was decidedly

picturesque with her resplendent black hair and white skin, in which the shadows were cold in contrast to the slightly pink tone of the lights, and also because Justine was always available whenever he had time and opportunity for painting. Age and hard work had both left their marks on her figure and taken some of the gloss off the health and beauty it had undoubtedly possessed in her youth. The abdomen had become rather too big and flabby and the tight stays had left their mark on the soft feminine skin, so that breast and hips were a little exaggerated. But Gauguin saw right through all this and penetrated to the great simple beauty of the living human form. Without in any way altering or improving what gave Justine's body its character, he painted a picture in which form and colour together made a harmonious whole. By her individuality and by the liberated charm of her nudity she awakened forces within him, as a man and as an observer of nature's fertile beauty in proportion, form, and colour.

With redoubled intensity Gauguin worked both at home and in his business, and the luck that attended him in the latter sphere did a good deal to strengthen his confidence in arriving at successful results in his painting; so that when the Salon des Indépendants was about to open, he did not hesitate to send in a number of pictures, among them the nude study of Justine.

And this time his contribution did not pass unnoticed. The nude study received such commendation from J. K. Huysmans as would never again fall
to his lot. At that time Huysmans, in addition to his
extremely contentious work as an author, had come
forward as the most zealous but at the same time the
most exacting champion of modern art, which gave
him an important place in the circle of which Pissarro was in a way the leader. His notice of Gauguin
is clear enough.

" Last year Gauguin exhibited for the first time.
A series of landscapes which were a watering-down
of works, still irresolute, by Pissarro. This year Gauguin makes his appearance with a canvas which is all
his own, one which reveals the incontestable temperament of a modern painter.

" It bears the title: *Study of the Nude.* . . . I do
not shrink from affirming that among contemporary
painters who have treated the nude, none has yet
given so vehement an expression of reality; and I
do not except Courbet, whose *Woman with a Parrot*
is no more true to life in its pose than in its flesh, or
Lefebvre's *Femme couchée*, or Cabanel's *Vénus à la
crème*. Courbet's paint is thickly laid on in the style
of Louis Philippe's time, whereas in the other more
modern painters the flesh quivers like a badly boiled
pudding. This, by the way, is the only difference between these artists. If Courbet had not introduced a
modern crinoline thrown over the end of the bed, his

woman might just as well have been entitled nymph or naiad. It is a trick of detail and nothing else that makes her a woman of today.

" In Gauguin's picture there is nothing of this sort; it is a girl of our day and a girl who does not exhibit herself to the gallery, who is neither voluptuous nor coquettish, who is quite simply mending her linen.

" And the skin is very expressive; it is not that smooth, sleek skin, without goose-flesh, without pouches or nodules, that skin which has been dipped in rosewater and ironed smooth, such as we see in other painters. It is skin which is flushed with blood, and beneath it nerves are quivering. And what truth there is in these forms, in the rather bulky abdomen sagging on to the thighs, in the swelling breasts with furrows under them, in the angular bend of the knee, and in the calluses on the wrists that are bending over the chemise!

" I am happy to be able to give my approval to a painter who, like myself, shows a pronounced distaste for mannequins with model pink breasts and hard narrow stomachs, mannequins who are ready to drop with so-called good taste, drawn after plaster casts according to receipt.

" Oh, the naked woman! Who has painted her really and perfectly, without deliberate prearrangement, without falsification of feature and flesh? Who has done it so that we can see the nationality of an

undressed woman, the age she belongs to, the calling she follows, and whether she is untouched or deflowered? Who has put her on canvas so real and alive that we have been able to dream of the life she leads, and almost to look for the marks of childbearing on her loins, to reconstruct her pains and her joys and to enter for a few minutes into her existence?

" In spite of the mythological titles and the fantastic garments in which he dresses his models, Rembrandt is to this day the only one who has painted the nude.

" In the absence of a genius like that wonderful painter it is to be desired that painters of talent like Gauguin should do for their age what van Rijn did for his. That they should find their way to the moments which make the nude possible, in bed, in the studio, in the amphitheatre, and in the bath, and re-create French women who were not built up of fragments, with arms belonging to one model, head and stomach to another, and in addition a tinkering counterfeit of the methods of the old masters.

" But, alas! these wishes have little chance of fulfilment while people are still shut up in galleries, filled with balderdash about art, and made to copy the antique. Nobody tells them that beauty is not uniform or unalterable, that it changes according to climate and century, that the Venus of Milo, to take one example, is neither more interesting nor more beautiful now than the ancient Indian statues that

are covered with tattoo-marks and wear feathered head-dresses. That neither the one nor the other is more than an expression of the ideal of beauty pursued by the different races, and that today it is not a question of hitting off the beautiful by means of a Venetian, Greek, Dutch, or Flemish rite, but of making an effort to distil the life of our own time in the world that surrounds us. And the beautiful is there, but the unfortunates who have rummaged around in the galleries of the Louvre cannot see on coming out into the street that girls are going past shedding a delightful charm of languishing youth to which the lack of oxygen in the city air lends a divine glamour. The nude is there, underneath the tight-fitting armour which clings to arms and thighs, modelling the form of hips and trunk and raising the breasts. A nudity which is the result of effort, delicate, refined, and vibrating. A civilized nudity the fatigued charm of which may reduce one to despair.

" Oh, I can't help laughing at the Winkelmanns and Sejerstedts who shed tears of admiration before Greek nudity and make bold to proclaim that beauty has permanently taken refuge in these masses of marble.

" And I repeat, Gauguin has been the first for ever so long to attempt to portray the woman of our time, and, in spite of the heaviness of the shadow thrown by the face across the model's breast, he has

been entirely successful, and he has accomplished a bold and completely independent work."

Gauguin was not left in doubt that Huysmans in any case took him quite seriously as an artist. It was true that the Impressionist circle looked upon Huysmans rather as a poet, considering him as something of a pioneer of the Impressionist movement in literature. His criticisms were therefore determined to a great extent by the mood of the moment and were apt to be capricious, and his language might be either trenchant or flowery. Not infrequently his pen ran away with him in one direction or the other. But he had always been a warm and enthusiastic champion of Manet, Degas, and Cézanne, the contemporary artists whom Gauguin valued most. His entirely unreserved appreciation of Gauguin's nude study and his comprehension of the meaning of the picture were calculated effectually to restore the painter's confidence in himself. He saw very clearly that as his work hitherto had been divided between two widely divergent interests, it was not very strange that most people, even those who knew him well, took a rather sceptical view of his painting. Who could guess that this department of his activity did not bring him any real satisfaction? The effective way in which he worked at it rather suggested the contrary. But it was a little painful nevertheless to notice that the friendly indulgence with which his

painting was received was almost always evoked by
the modest attitude he himself usually adopted when
speaking of his art, especially in the presence of those
artists who really meant something to him. Therefore Huysmans's powerful appeal to him as an artist
did him good. It came in a way as a surprise, and its
effect was therefore the stronger.

His attitude was no longer quite so modest; he
gave his opinion more firmly, as the direct and confident expression of his personal conception of the
nature of painting. The stockbroker retired more
into the background and the artist began to assert
himself.

Mette was the last to discover this, she was now so
used to Paul's downright way of expressing his opinion and to its always differing from that of other
people; and she had quite ceased to pay any attention
to his hobby, especially after he had left off using her
as a model. Besides, she had enough on her hands
with looking after the children, and another was
expected. But her friends of both sexes were more
observant of her husband's rather curious manner.
And particularly a couple of Norwegian painters
who had lately come on a visit, after her sister and
her husband, the Norwegian painter Fritz Thaulow,
had settled in Paris for a time. They liked the lively,
sociable, and witty Mette Gauguin, but thought her
husband the banker a queer fish, inclined to be dis-
agreeable, especially when the talk was of art, as it

FROM THE RUE CARCEL

1881

WINTER IN THE RUE CARCEL
1881

was very often. The Norwegian painters had been studying under Léon Bonnat, whom they naturally admired, and one of them, Christian Skredsvig, had been awarded the gold medal at the Salon. One of the first occasions when he met Gauguin was at the Thaulows'. As usual Mette was the centre of a lively conversation, so Skredsvig, who was an amiable nature and in great spirits over his luck at the Salon, wanted to be pleasant to Mette Gauguin's husband, who seemed rather depressed and ill at ease in the company of these artists who had done well at the Salon, and to bring him into the general conversation. " Splendid exhibition this year, lots of good pictures and not a few masterly ones, but Bonnat's *Christ Crucified* towers above them all. A little too realistic perhaps, rather brutal, but wonderfully painted, strong, manly in its expression! What do you think, Monsieur Gauguin? "

" I? I only saw one picture in the Salon, and that was Manet's."

Short and sweet, a smack in the face for the Norwegian painter, who was in the best of humours and only trying to be civil to the husband of his excellent friend Fritz's sister-in-law. Who would have guessed that that man of all others should hold such decided opinions about art?

A little later he saw him go round the studio by himself with a big three-branched candlestick in his hand, studying Thaulow's pictures. He expressed his

opinion by a shrug of the shoulders. His way of showing it was neither pleasant nor polite, but the almost unanimous enthusiasm this company showed for everything connected with the Salon irritated him so that he reacted rather curtly, wishing thereby to hint that other views might be justified, even if they came from a banker. It was excessively uncomfortable to feel that he was between the devil and the deep sea, to have clear evidence that he would not be understood in any quarter if he cut himself adrift and gave up his position in the bank. Even the worthy Schuffenecker would be flabbergasted and would declare that if he himself left the bank and took to painting it would amount to much the same. His chances were not so good and he knew how to economize, but as for Gauguin with his habits and his prospects — it was sheer madness. Gauguin had a firm belief in himself as an artist, but the hostility with which he felt he would be surrounded alarmed him. He therefore kept the matter to himself and it impaired his working powers, with results that were specially noticeable in his painting.

And in fact the pictures he exhibited at the Salon des Indépendants in the year following his success had an extremely unfavourable reception from Huysmans. The tone of his very brief notice was slighting in its condescension, and this irritated Gauguin. The irritation did much to arouse his dormant consciousness that art demanded a final choice on his

part, and at the end of the year he announced to his
wife that he had left the bank.

In reality this came as a complete surprise to
Mette. She found it perfectly insane. All her former
ideas about Paul were swept away. No doubt there
were traits in his character which had always been
alien to her. She sometimes joked about them, but as
a rule she let them pass as things that concerned him
alone; never had they led to any serious conflict between them. But now the alien element had come to
the surface; it was a new husband that faced her and
he was not to be trifled with. And she knew him
well enough to be sure he would not say one thing
today and another thing tomorrow. On the contrary,
he could be unreasonably obstinate when once he had
made a resolution, but she was bound to acknowledge
that he scarcely ever did so without due consideration. The only hope was that he was overworked.
He could not possibly be quite normal. And this view
received animated support on all sides, even among
Paul Gauguin's artist friends. Pissarro especially
was dismayed to find that the good-natured instruc-
tion with which he had helped a talented and interested business man had taken such an unfortunate turn. But of course it was quite on the cards that
when once he was left in peace to devote himself entirely to his painting, Gauguin would very soon be
brought to see that his ability as a painter was quite
insufficient to enable him to reach his extremely am-

bitious aims. For the present there was no imminent danger. He had put by enough capital for them to live on for some time to come, and Calzado promised that Gauguin's place should be kept open for him, whenever he chose to return.

Gauguin was the only one who was quite clear about the significance of the resolution he had taken, but at the same time he was the only one who took an optimistic view of the chances it offered him and absolutely the only one who was quite confident that his powers were equal to the highest aims. He was not particularly economical or practical in money matters — gave them little thought, in fact — and Mette was much the same. If now and again she preached economy for the future, especially considering their rather numerous flock of children, he made a joke of it; their fine, well-grown children didn't want many clothes now, and in all their nakedness they were worth a fortune to him as a painter. When Gauguin talked about the future he did so quite calmly, and in speaking of his art he showed no sign of fanaticism, so that in a way his wife was taken in. The man before her was too sensible and too well balanced to embark on any adventure and pursue it to the bitter end. Sooner or later he would break loose from the narrow range of ideas in which she and others thought it abnormal for a man of his mould and talents to be so entirely caught. For this reason and because she was a brave woman

GAUGUIN'S SON JEAN
1881

STILL LIFE
1882

with an unshakable trust that fate would never be hard on her and the children, she took no serious precautions in view of possible future difficulties. Even when in the early summer she discovered that she was again to have a child, she had no misgivings. She made up her mind that if it was a boy he should be called Paul — an appeal to her husband's common sense.

It was not until December, after the birth of her son Paul, that a shadow of anxiety crossed her mind. Her husband told her that they must leave their home in the rue Carcel and move to Rouen. For the time being, he had no chance in Paris; his friends turned their backs on him and the art dealers regretted that they had no more room for hatching out new eggs; the nest was full and the lately hatched chickens claimed their attention. It was just as well to leave expensive Paris and wait for better times in a cheaper place. Besides, the air of Paris did not suit him, it was so infected with art and artists' chatter about Impressionism, which did not interest him as a movement. He wanted to try new lines more in conformity with decorative simplification and far removed from the Impressionists' involved combinations of effects of light and movement. And at the same time he wanted to achieve a style of portraiture based more on the naked facts and on entirely primitive characteristics than on the effect produced by the subject in his surroundings. Where and how he

was to do this he did not know, but at any rate it would not be in Paris or by the aid of the excellent theories with which Pissarro had inoculated him. No doubt they had served him well, but now they clung to him like a strange perfume in one's clothes which has become insupportable and which one must get rid of. Away from Paris, that was the only thing. Let oneself be carried along by the river, away from the bewildering noise of the city, nearer to the sea, with its vast featureless expanse.

But the stay in Rouen was not of long duration. Even though he had attained to greater simplicity in his motives and a purer, less complicated colouring, the atmosphere was much the same. It was dominated by his family life, which he had himself created, but in other conditions and with other assumptions. It no longer gave him a basis for his art and he was unable to transform it. He was beginning to be a stranger to the woman in it. He was disrooted, and restlessly searched for a means of escape. And Mette noticed it; she pressed the child she was still nursing closer to her and called him with plaintive tenderness *Petit Pola.* To her the meaning of life was in the children. They entirely dominated her emotional life and had always done so to such an extent that she had never really tried to penetrate to her husband's confidence and therefore had never attached any importance to what she felt to be the alien element in him. But now she could not avoid

seeing it. Her practical sense and her active spirit were awakened, her maternal feeling was translated into material claims; but how were they to be satisfied? The attitude adopted by her circle of friends left no doubt in her that Paul's decision was bound to land them in misfortune and she felt how unpractical and difficult he was in the matter of forming connections, a thing which to her seemed so easy and obvious. But as things had now shaped themselves France had become practically impossible; better to move to Denmark before it was too late. There she would feel secure, and if the last remnant of their savings should be spent before Paul had returned to his senses, she could always turn her hand to something.

Gauguin himself raised no difficulty; on the contrary, the idea appealed to him. In August 1884, eight months after their move to Rouen, the whole family with all its possessions embarked for Denmark. Only Gauguin's own pictures and some of the most valuable paintings from his collection were left behind in France for all eventualities. In order to strengthen their finances and to improve his position in the eyes of the Gad family he had secured an agency for the sale of tarpaulin.

CHAPTER 4

THE reception given to Gauguin in Denmark was not remarkable for cordiality. The courtesy and friendliness shown him out of consideration for Mette by her family and her old circle of friends could not long conceal from him the reservations they made in the case of a man who not only appeared to them foreign in language and manner, but was also somewhat insusceptible to the tone of ordinary social intercourse. All the simple habits and amusements which help to make daily life smooth and agreeable seemed indifferent to him. To them he appeared as a man whose serious opinions, whose strong personal views and convictions, bore no reasonable relation to his very uncertain and equivocal position in society. Salesman and artist was not exactly a combination calculated to inspire much respect in the members of the Gad family.

These good-looking, ready-witted people were accustomed to deal with all classes easily and in a fitting

manner. Family feeling and tradition had in a short time established themselves among these well-grown people, and they aimed at good positions in the service of the State and simple but substantial domestic relations.

They were inclined to look down on business, and their interest in art was entirely determined by the degree of appreciation it enjoyed in the eyes of society. They were straightforward people who reckoned with facts; backed by these they were ready to give a rapid and self-assured judgment about everything and everybody.

Facts did not speak in favour of Gauguin, and it was not long before the family discovered that he preferred to follow his own narrow paths rather than the straight, broad road of realities. Or else they looked upon him as the master of a boat, which in their opinion he was sailing with a faulty compass and without an anchor. Entirely irresponsible, he trusted too much in himself, without any regard for the passengers he had on board.

And unfortunately Gauguin himself became aware that he was in shallow waters and had entered a channel that would not take him into the open sea. It was with no friendly eye that he regarded the simple, smiling scenes of Denmark. Here was little space and many fences; and behind the fences were neighbours who had to be considered. This was done with cool and capable deliberation, and with much

knowledge of human nature. It gave warmth to the home and the soil, to the whole country of Denmark.

Mette had not lost this strong national sentiment during her ten years' sojourn in France, in company with a husband in whom this feeling was far from unmixed. Gauguin now saw his home becoming more and more estranged from him without his being able to prevent it. But, being very conscientious, it pained him, and he knew that he would never be able entirely to free himself from this pain. Nor could he get rid of the outward appearance of irresponsibility and recklessness entailed by acting according to the dictates of his real conscience. This lack of understanding made him far more bitter than did the fact that no one showed the slightest interest in the work in which he was entirely absorbed, and his bitterness was specially directed against Denmark, where his guilty conscience had begun to take root, and was destined to grow more firmly as time went on.

In surroundings so foreign and unfavourable it was quite natural that Gauguin should begin to lose his taste for working at his art, and his business agency very soon proved to be useless. He had neither the address nor the patience required to obtain successful results. The situation in which he found himself was in reality a fateful one. And to make it worse his finances threatened disaster, so that Mette had to start giving lessons in French in order to contribute. Here her former good connections, especially

GAUGUIN'S SON CLOVIS

COPENHAGEN, 1884

LANDSCAPE

COPENHAGEN, 1885

with Estrup, were of great service, so that she soon made a name as a teacher, particularly among young men preparing for the diplomatic service.

At home Gauguin was forced more and more into the background; he and his painting materials had to be relegated to a little inner room, as the drawing-room was required for his wife and her pupils, many of whom belonged to the Danish nobility. A small skylight was all he had to work by and he had no opportunity of using models. The only model he had was himself, so here he sat alone during the long winter months, painting his own portrait. His powerful, animated face has grown rigid in profound reflection, his gaze is introspective under the heavy eyelids, and his full lips are compressed. Silence reigns in the room, only disturbed now and then by distant merriment — Mette and her pupils. Within him a violent revolt is stirring, but the hand that holds the brush does not tremble; it is calm and sure — not yet entirely liberated, still somewhat restrained by the strict schooling it has gone through. Gauguin knows this, but he also knows that the time is not far distant when it will be freed. His artistic conscience is so clear and strong that everything which stands between him and his goal must give way. And the day will come when he will be able to put everything on its feet again. He has no distrust of others and none at all of his own gifts. An indomitable optimist in spite of everything, unsuspecting where others are con-

—*85*—

cerned, a bad judge of human nature, but wise, sensible, and clear-sighted in his judgment of himself. A primitive nature with powerful instincts, but at the same time refined and distinguished by conflicting characteristics inherited from different races.

" My political opinions? I have none. But with universal suffrage one ought to have some.

" I am a republican, because I consider that the community must live in peace. In France the majority is definitely republican. And, for that matter, so few people appreciate what is great and noble that a democratic government is desirable.

" Long live democracy! It is the only thing. Philosophically I believe the Republic to be a deception (painter's expression) and I have a horror of deceptions. So I become an anti-republican again (philosophically considered). Spontaneously, instinctively, without reflection, I love nobility, beauty, refined taste, and the old motto: *Noblesse oblige*. I like good manners, politeness, even that of Louis XIV's time.

" Thus I am, intuitively and without knowing why, an aristocrat — as an artist.

" Art is only for the few. In itself it ought to be noble. It is only the big men who have protected art, from instinct, from sense of duty, possibly from arrogance. Never mind why. They have caused great and beautiful things to be produced. Kings and popes treated an artist on an equal footing so to speak. The democrats, bankers, ministers, and art critics give

themselves the air of protectors, but do not protect; they deal with art as if they were buying fish in the market. And then you expect an artist to be a republican.

" Here you have my political opinions in a few words. I consider that every man has a right to live and to live well in the community in proportion to his output of work. The artist cannot live. Therefore society is criminal and badly organized. Some people say: the artist makes useless things, but the workman, the manufacturer, in short everyone who provides the country with a work which can be paid for, enriches the nation. When he is dead he leaves something behind him of value. And I will go further: he alone enriches the nation. And this is not the case with the broker or the business man. A hundred francs circulate in a variety of small coins. The broker makes them pass from hand to hand and into his own pocket. The nation still has a hundred francs, not a centime more."

It was now becoming increasingly clear to Gauguin that his firm determination to continue his career as an artist would relentlessly force him out of the world in which he had hitherto been living and out of the home he had made for himself. Although fully convinced that this was only a transitional phase, he would have to begin again from the beginning and alone, until the day when he would be strong enough to give proof of the justification of his

existence. But there was no question of a breach with
his family; he would maintain contact with them,
they were a part of his ego and they had a place in
all his future prospects.

His leave-taking with Mette was a calm one.
They parted without tears or assurances, he to carve
his way, while she stayed behind in her native land
to keep together what existed. She agreed with him
that this was best for them both. And he took Clovis
with him when in June 1885 he returned to France.
He was relieved and emancipated, had got rid of a
burden of self-reproach which stood in the way of
his initiative and paralysed his working powers now
that he had every use for them in order to break with
his whole artistic past and make a name for himself
as a painter; but at the same time the magnitude of
the sacrifice made him bitter and disappointed. His
self-confidence had received a severe shock. His un-
compromising uprightness had to choose between
failing in the duty he felt he owed to his family and
being false to himself. He had bitter experience that
the law of bourgeois society knows no pity, but
judges one's personal accomplishment from the financial point of view, and that on that score he was
utterly rejected. He had already suspected this in
France, but in Denmark it was made clear to him in
a cool and downright fashion, and not least by the
family of the woman who was dear to him as his wife
and the mother of his children. No serious difficulties

were placed in the way of his project, no conditions were imposed; it was he himself who wished to take his son with him, and yet it felt like a flight. And it left a wound in his mind which was hard to heal.

" I hate Denmark with all my heart, its climate and its people. That there is some good in it is incontestable. Whereas for twenty-five years Norway and Sweden have flooded French picture-galleries with their imitations of anything that smells bad but looks pretty, Denmark, ashamed of her reverse at the Paris Exhibition of 1878, has been thinking things over and collecting herself. This has led to the growth of a Danish art which is very personal and deserving of the most serious attention, and I am happy to be able to praise it in this connection. It may be a good thing to study French art and even that of other countries, but only in order to gain a better insight into oneself.

" They played a curious practical joke on me in Copenhagen. I, who never push myself forward, was pressingly invited by a gentleman in the name of an art union to exhibit my works in their gallery. And I allowed myself to be persuaded. I looked in on the opening day and to my indescribable astonishment was told that the exhibition had been closed by order at noon. Impossible to get any information; everybody's mouth was shut. Went on to the influential man who had invited me. The footman received me with the statement that his master had gone into the

country and would not be back for a long time. As you see, Denmark is a charming country.

" It must be admitted all the same that in Denmark a great deal is spent on education and on the sciences, especially medicine. The hospital in Copenhagen may be said to be one of the finest buildings of its kind, both in size and in its internal arrangement, which is first-rate; that honour is due to them. All the more as apart from this I have only a sad tale to relate. And yet I am forgetting that their houses are excellently arranged, with a view to both warmth and fresh air, and that the town is handsome in summer. It must also be said that people always receive their guests in the dining-room and that the food is excellent. It is always there and that helps you to pass the time. So you have to get used to the kind of conversation you hear every day: ' Coming from a great country you must find everything here much behind the times. We are so small. What do you think of Copenhagen, our museums, etc.? They are not of much account.' And all this is said to make you say just the opposite. And you do so, presumably, out of sheer politeness. You don't forget your manners.

" Talking about the museums. To tell the truth there is no collection of paintings, apart from a few pictures of the old Danish school, landscapes as elaborate as Meissonier's and some clever pictures of small boats. Let us hope things are better today. There is a monumental building erected solely for

their great sculptor Thorvaldsen, a Dane who lived
and died in Italy. I have seen it, I looked at it till my
head buzzed. The Greek pantheon has turned Scan-
dinavian and has then been scrubbed to make it
Protestant. The Venuses cast down their eyes and
modestly drape themselves in wet towels. And the
nymphs dance a jig. Yes, I assure you, they're dancing a jig. Just look at their feet.

" In Europe they talk about the great Thorvaldsen, but they haven't seen him. His famous lion is the
only thing of his that can be seen by tourists in Swit-
zerland! A stuffed Danish dog. If I were to say this
in Denmark I know I should be banned irreclaimably
for daring to insult the greatest Danish sculptor.
There are many other things that make me hate Denmark, but they are private reasons which one ought
to keep to oneself.

" But now let me introduce you to a home such as
one seldom sees nowadays, the home of a count belonging to the most distinguished Danish nobility.
The salon is square, hung with two huge pieces of
German tapestry, as wonderful as you could wish to
see. They were specially executed for this family.
Over two of the doors are views of Venice, by Tur-
ner; the chairs are carved with the family coat of
arms, the tables inlaid, the hangings are in keeping.
Wonderful art everywhere.

" You are announced and received; you take your
seat on a pouf covered with red plush and shaped like

a snail's shell, and on a handsome table you see a tea-cloth that cost a few francs at the Bon Marché, a photograph album and flower vases in the same style. Vandals!!

" Leading out of the drawing-room is a very hand-some gallery. It contains the collection of pictures. Portrait of Rembrandt's mother and so on. There is a musty smell; nobody ever comes here. The family prefers the chapel, where they read the Bible and where everything oppresses you like a stone weigh-ing on your heart.

" I must admit that the system of getting engaged in Denmark is good, because it doesn't bind either of the parties (you change your fiancée as you change your shirt), and yet the whole thing has a semblance of love, liberty, and morality. If you're engaged you can go about together as much as you like, you can even travel together; the cloak of betrothal covers all. You play with everything, except the one thing; this teaches both parties not to forget themselves and do anything silly. With each of her engagements the bird loses a lot of little feathers, but they grow again without anybody noticing it. Very practical, these Danes. — Take a sip of it, but don't lose your head. If you do, you may easily regret it, for remember, the Danish woman is extraordinarily practical. Bear in mind that it's a small country where you have to be careful. Even as children they are taught to say:

'Papa, we must have some money; you'll have to turn out your pockets, poor papa.'

" I hate the Danes. . . .

" These people have the most extraordinary ideas of modesty. Thus every owner of a villa on the shore of the Sound has his little hut for dressing and un- dressing, and the main road runs between the villas and the bathing-huts.

" Men and women bathe separately and at differ- ent hours. They bathe naked, and the rule is that peo- ple going along the road don't see anything. I confess that, being of a curious turn, I sinned against this rule one day as the wife of a minister was calmly wading out into the water. I will also confess that her white body, exposed down to the calves, was ex- tremely effective. Her little girl followed her, and she turned round and discovered me. ' Mamma! ' Mamma turned, got a fright, and made for the hut again. And now, after having shown me her back, she gave me a view of her front. Once more I must confess that at that distance the effect was pretty good. There was a scandal. Fancy! he stopped and looked at us! "

THE countenance which Paris presented to Gauguin on his return was grey and expressionless. And he was not one of those who seek to evoke either smiles or tears. To look for help and consolation was not his

way. Least of all now that he was facing the turning-point in his life, when he had to concentrate entirely on himself and liberate himself from all influences, could he be subject to any bonds of gratitude or indebtedness. The only one he really wanted to see was Schuffenecker, who at once received him with effusive cordiality, inspired by obvious admiration which, together with his wife's warm and honest friendliness, did Gauguin good. But neither Schuffenecker's own paintings nor his glowing enthusiasm for Impressionism had anything to say to him. And he told his friend straight out that Impressionism was far too restricted. The great importance it attached to the problem of light and to the direct impression left little room for expressing the primitive and plastic beauty of the human body, or the monumental quality and the rhythmical decorative force in nature. Impressionism was only fit for interiors; it had only the eye as its medium, whereas thought and feeling also had claims to express themselves in pictorial form. Both colour and plasticity are capable of expressing the many moods of the mind when ideas force themselves upon us. " You want Symbolism," suggested Schuffenecker. " No, what I want is that human beings and nature, primitive and unadorned, shall unite to give an image of the harmony and beauty by which every civilized society tries to express its vital instinct. Symbolism is only a covert expression of inhibited vitality. There is something

LANDSCAPE
DIEPPE, 1885

LANDSCAPE

empty about symbols — the word always reminds me of cymbals. Both the Symbolists and the Impressionists are trying to find their artistic form through ingenuity. I am going to try to find *my* form in the simplest and to me most natural way. I know I have a right to do this, but let me have walls. I'm not going to be modest, because I don't want to be an ass. As yet I haven't got there; but be sure that will come and then I shall be understood. Christianity and civilization together have tried to abolish man's belief in himself and in the beauty of the primitive instincts, so that this has become a myth, but as such it is alive in every human being. I want to restore the myth to reality."

To Schuffenecker, who belonged to a set with very different and restricted views about " Art for Art's sake," all that Gauguin said was fairly problematical; he admired him and believed in him, but for his own part he saw no prospect for an artistic tendency like Gauguin's. And he knew and understood enough to tell him that it would not find a fertile soil among those artists who influenced the new movement in art, which was just beginning to make headway with certain critics and art dealers and through them might reach the buying public.

And unfortunately it was very soon apparent that Gauguin's strong conviction would not suffice to carry him to his goal in the circumstances he had created for himself. Winter was coming on, and he

was obliged to move from one place to another with his little six-year-old son, before he found a modest apartment in the rue Cail. His whole baggage was one trunk with such clothes as were barely necessary for himself and the boy. He slept on a mattress on the floor, wrapt in a travelling plaid; for the child he had hired a bed.

He had no good news to send to his family in Denmark; nor were the letters he received from there very encouraging. As yet Mette had not quite settled down to her position as the support of a family and she was full of anxiety. Both were accustomed to reveal their thoughts and feelings to each other, but at this distance it was not easy for one to judge fairly of the other's position.

Bitterness often gained the upper hand in his letters, prompted by the hard realities he forced a little six-year-old to share with him.

" I have received your letter which gives such a mournful description of your situation; I have done my best to see things from your point of view and I confess they do not seem so bad to me. You are living in *your house*, decently furnished, surrounded by your children, working at a strenuous job, but one which you like; you meet people and as you are fond of the society of women and of your compatriots, you have some opportunities of indulging this taste. You enjoy the advantages of marriage without being

troubled with a husband. What more do you want, except a little more money? Many others are in a like case.

"Whereas I am driven from my home, and how am I living! — between four walls, a bed, a table, no fire, no company. Clovis is heroic; when we sit together of an evening at our table before a bit of bread and a slice of ham, he never thinks of the dainties he used to be given. He says nothing, asks for nothing, not even leave to play, and then he goes to bed. That is his life day by day; his heart and his brains are now those of a grown-up person. He is growing fast, but is not very well. . . ."

But a correspondence of this sort is dangerous. So much is read between the lines. Perhaps the words were meant, but they are quickly forgotten. The intervals between the letters are long.

"You are quite wrong to think I have been angry. I have grown a very thick skin and have nothing left but disgust with all that has happened. That the children are forgetting me has now become a matter of indifference. Besides, I don't see any possibility of ever seeing them again, and God grant that death may take us all. That would be the best present he could make us. . . .

"Don't worry about my forgiveness for your faults; I have forgotten all that long ago; even your sister, who was the wickedest and stupidest in the

whole business, is now to me a woman like any other. I have always made the mistake of believing in virtue. All is forgotten."

Gauguin was in a bad way; he was working hard, but it was a strain on him. His conscience stood between him and his life's aim; it spoke severely and was always beside him in the person of the gentle, patient, fair-haired boy with the innocent blue eyes which saw and understood that his father was suffering.

And one day Clovis was taken ill with smallpox. Limp and burning with fever the strong, brave boy lay dozing in his bed. A rapid decision was called for: should he lay down his arms, surrender? His conscience spoke with two voices. He could not do it; better to take any job he could get.

" *My dear Mette,*

" Necessity knows no law; sometimes too it makes a man overstep the bounds imposed on him by society. When the little one was attacked by smallpox I had 20 centimes in my pocket and for three days we had been living on credit — *dry bread*. In my despair I had the idea of offering myself as a bill-poster to an advertising company. My respectable appearance made the Director laugh, but I told him very seriously that I had a sick child and that I wanted work. So I have been posting bills for 5 francs a day; during this time Clovis was confined to his

bed by the fever, and in the evening I returned to nurse him. This has been going on for three weeks, and today the Director of the company has taken me on as superintendent and secretary at 200 francs a month. It seems they have found me intelligent and I believe that in a year's time I shall have a better situation. They are negotiating at this moment with Spain about establishing an agency at Madrid, where I am to be appointed manager with a salary of 300 francs a month, free lodging and 20 per cent on the returns. Besides, the company is a rich one, has for 30 years been carrying on a business which is likely to be extended. So that is a future which may have better things in store for me. The present is still a hard time, but there is encouragement in it and it is a great deal better than the past.

" Your Danish self-esteem will be hurt at having a bill-poster husband. But what do you ask for? everybody can't have talent. Don't worry about the little one, he is getting better and better and I have no idea of sending him back to you; on the contrary, I *count* on taking others of the children as my poster business grows. I have a right to do so, as you know.

" You ask me to answer in the same gentle tone in which you write, so I have gone through very calmly all the letters in which you tell me very cool-headedly and, be it said, with much common sense that I loved you once but that now you are no more than Mother and not wife, etc. These memories are very pleasant

to me, but they have one very great disadvantage —
they leave me with no illusions for the future. It
ought not to astonish you therefore if one day, when
my circumstances have improved, I find a woman
who may be to me something besides a mother,
etc.

" I know very well that you look on me as devoid
of all charm, but that just pricks me on to prove the
contrary. Perhaps in Spain that will be easier. Meanwhile go on as you are doing, holding your head high
before the world, inspired by your duties, with a
clear conscience. For that matter, there is only one
crime, adultery. With that exception everything is
right and proper. It is not just that you should be
driven out of your house, but it is reasonable that I
should be driven out of mine. So you won't think it
mean if I make another home for myself. And in it
I shall be able to post bills. Everyone has his own
way of blushing.

" Remember me kindly to your family.

" *Your husband,*

" *Paul* "

Gauguin could not take his actual position altogether seriously. With scathing irony he insists on
the absurdity of earning his living by taking on a job
far inferior to what he would have been entitled to
if only he had been willing to sacrifice the idea which
alone could release the tension in his mind and bring

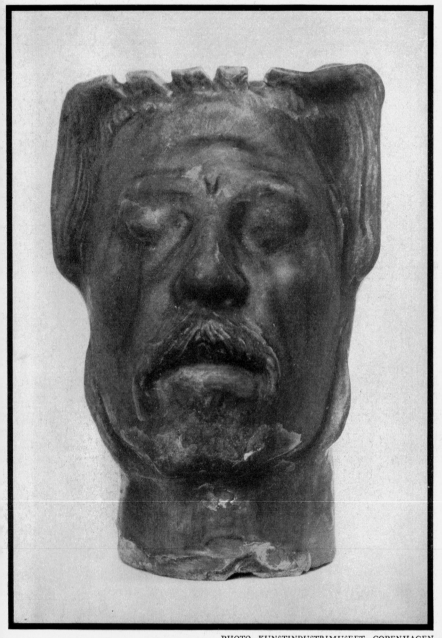

PORTRAIT OF HIMSELF, CERAMIC
1886

into play the powers he really possessed. So far down
did he have to go in order to prove to himself and
others how insignificant were the financial demands
of the moment compared with his real aims. Although what he had produced in the last four years
did not satisfy him, he sent in nineteen pictures and
a piece of wood-carving to the Salon des Indépendants in 1886, to show that his determination to continue as an artist was unchanged; but he was quite
prepared for a cool reception. He was himself well
aware that he was still under the sway of too many
influences, as well as fortuitous circumstances, which
had set their mark on his art. All this he would have
to shake off. He must get away from Paris, that cold
place for a poor man of many wants, away from
the crushing responsibility which weighed upon him
continually, so that he could concentrate and work
in peace. When Clovis was quite recovered he placed
him in a pension outside Paris, where he left him for
a time. He took his departure, but not as a bill-poster,
nor yet to Spain. It was as a painter with no financial
prospects that he left for Pont-Aven in Brittany, in
the hope that the simplicity of the scenery and the
primitive nature of the people would answer the intentions of his art.

And he was not altogether mistaken. In many
ways Brittany answered his expectations, but with
his inquiring mind and his thoroughness it took him
time to get to work and to exploit to the full that

simplification in his painting which he aimed at in
agreement with his feeling for nature.

" To tell the truth, I haven't the facility of comprehension that others find without effort at the tips
of their brushes. They get out of the train, take up
their palette, and in a second they've got a sunlight
effect. When it is dry it goes to the Luxembourg and
is signed Carolus Durand. I don't admire the painting, but I do the man. He is so sure and calm, and I
am so uncertain and anxious. At every fresh place I
come to I must have time to get acclimatized, to get
to know the nature of the trees, the plants, the scenery
in short, which is so varied and capricious and is
never willing to yield itself up to you."

Even if the work itself went rather slowly, the
idea was taking shape with growing conviction in
Gauguin's mind. At the same time he was becoming more restful, his financial difficulties no longer
wounded his pride so severely or preyed on his self-
confidence. The calm and simple life he was leading
made him forget his bitterness. All the unfriendli-
ness and indifference he had met with in Paris was
swept away by the Bretons' hospitality and interested
kindliness. He began to see himself and his art in a
bolder light, more strongly armed against the arbitrary blows of existence. His fighting spirit was
aroused.

" The other day I had news of Clovis; it seems
that they are getting very fond of him at the pension

and that he is as right as a trivet. I miss him very much and if I had had the money I should have brought him here. Poor little chap, he won't have any holidays, but in this world one can only do what one can. . . .

" Strange how well I feel in the midst of all these worries; I have never worked so hard. When my fall comes it will probably come with a crash. . . ."

And with the improvement in his spirits he began to make plans. His energy and new-born optimism once more made him restless and impatient to strike a blow for his financial existence, which could only be done in Paris. And late in the autumn he returned thither. He succeeded in selling a small picture from his collection; earlier attempts had been fruitless, as he would never submit to be cheated by the art dealers and let things go at any price. He starved rather than sell at a ridiculous price his own pictures or those he had of other painters, and therefore was left with the greater part of his collection on his hands. But everyone knew he was in difficulties, so he could neither borrow money nor sell his things reasonably.

This time, however, he did manage to sell a little picture by the Dutch painter Jongkind for three hundred and fifty francs. He brought his boy home from the pension and began to work at pottery, in order if possible to earn a little in this way. But after a couple of months he was just where he started.

Clovis was sent back to the pension, he himself was without a sou, only the richer by a few paintings and some pottery of his own making. That winter Gauguin met for the first time an artist who not only was his comrade in misfortune, but whom he felt to be achieving really great artistic aims. But whereas he himself made great demands on existence, Vincent van Gogh accepted his fate with the patience of an angel. And van Gogh had a great attraction for Gauguin both as a man and as a painter.

" The Pink Shrimps.

" Winter of '86.

" The snow has begun to fall. You can keep that about the shroud; it is just snow. Poor people are in a bad way. Those who have something are apt to forget that. Along the rue Lepic in our beloved city of Paris the pedestrians are hurrying faster than usual on this December day. No temptation to loiter. Among them a poor shivering fellow in a strange get-up is hurrying towards the outer boulevards. He is wrapped in a goatskin coat; wears a fur cap, probably rabbit; has a bristly red beard. Some sort of a drover. But don't be in too much of a hurry; cold as it is, take a second look at that white and well-shaped hand, those clear and childlike blue eyes. A poor devil, sure enough. His name is Vincent van Gogh. He slips into a shop full of Negro weapons, old iron,

and cheap oil paintings. Poor artist! You have put your soul into this picture you are going to sell — a little still-life. Pink shrimps on a piece of pink paper.

" ' I suppose you couldn't give me something for this picture to help with the rent? '

" ' The deuce! My friend, customers are getting difficult; they come here wanting to buy cheap Millets. And then, you must know, your paintings are not particularly cheerful. The Renaissance is what goes on the boulevards. But they say you have talent, so I'll do something for you. Here you are, five francs.'

" The round coin rang on the counter and van Gogh took it without a murmur, thanked the man, and went out. Wearily he made his way along the rue Lepic. As he approached his lodging a poor woman just let out of St. Lazare smiled — at the painter. She thought he might be a customer.

" The fine white hand was withdrawn from the top-coat. Van Gogh was fond of reading — he pictured to himself some ' fille Elisa,' and the five francs became the property of the unfortunate. Quickly, as though ashamed of his charity, he fled with an empty stomach.

" Sequel!

" A day will come, and I see it as though it were today. We enter room No. 9 at the auctioneer's, where a collection of paintings is being sold. ' 400

francs for The Pink Shrimps — 450 — 500. Now, gentlemen, it's worth more than that! ' Nobody bids more. Gone — The Pink Shrimps by van Gogh."

And Gauguin was not mistaken. He saw that the kind blue eyes which followed him attentively as he expounded his artistic ideas were bright with intelligence, faith, and temperament. Different as were their characters, they had an irresistible attraction for one another. As artists both were strong; one by virtue of his conviction, the other in his faith that the cause they supported would win through some day. Van Gogh was five years younger than Gauguin and, like the latter, had not taken up painting until he was thirty. He had only been painting for four years or so when he met Gauguin and was thus himself in the experimental stage, though he began from an entirely different angle. While the Dutchman van Gogh sought his inspiration in French art and to some extent in impressionism, which he interpreted in his own way according to a simple and in many ways natural and primitive train of thought, Gauguin was trying to free himself from all this and was led by an instinct towards the primitive. Van Gogh was an ardent and impulsive fanatic; Gauguin was cool and clear-headed in his fanaticism. Van Gogh was extremely receptive; Gauguin more disposed to reflection. But these two very different characters were united by a common feeling of being isolated

from the artistic movement of the day, since they both pursued an aim which in many ways differed entirely from the view of art which now at last was on the point of achieving success after a struggle of nearly twenty years. And they not merely differed, they opposed this view, and in reality Gauguin came to feel more of a stranger in his native city than the Dutchman van Gogh, who in the course of a year had taught himself to speak French perfectly. While this isolation meant little to the unassuming van Gogh, to Gauguin it was a tragedy which wore down his health and made Paris more and more of a hell for him. And yet Paris held all his expectations; it was his city, the place where he was one day to occupy the position to which he was entitled as artist and man. This made it bitter to feel that Paris had turned its back on him. No doubt he could count Schuffenecker and a few of his set as his admirers, but of all those he met, van Gogh was the only one for whom he himself could show any admiration and who was able really to encourage his artistic efforts.

For these reasons he determined to go far away and seek a simpler existence in primitive conditions. And he chose Martinique in the hope of finding what he wanted.

" Next month I am leaving for America by the mail-boat of April 10th. I can't continue this shattering and enfeebling existence any longer and I am going to try all I can to have a clear conscience. . . .

" Why do you leave me so long without a letter? It seems to me I have a right to hear from you from time to time. My letters are not very gay, but what can you expect? I have so much to go through that it is almost beyond human endurance. Before leaving for the unknown I should be very glad to have your news, as I am not able to kiss you good-bye."

And it wounded his pride deeply to have to hand over Clovis to the care of Mette; he scarcely alluded to it, and only in vague terms. His affairs were in such a mess that it was impossible to get them straightened out.

" I was expecting your letter impatiently, as I leave Saint-Nazaire on April 10th; you see I have no time to lose.

" You seem to have misunderstood my letter about Clovis; you must find *someone who will take charge of him on the journey*. I am leaving with *just* enough for the voyage and I shall arrive in America penniless. What do I expect to do there? I don't yet know myself. You understand that without the sinews of war it is pretty difficult; but what I want above all is to escape from Paris, which is a wilderness for a poor man. My name as an artist is growing day by day, but in the meanwhile I sometimes go three days without a meal, which is destructive not only of my health but of my *energy*. The latter I aim to restore, and I am going to Panama to live like a *savage*. I know of a little island (Taboga) about three miles

FROM MARTINIQUE
1887

PHOTO, NY CARLSBERG GLYPTOTEK, COPENHAGEN

FROM MARTINIQUE. 1887

off the coast of Panama, in the Pacific. It is almost uninhabited, free and very fertile. I am taking my colours and brushes and I am going to recruit in solitude. The air of the place is very healthful, and as for food, one can get fish and fruit for a mere trifle."

Gauguin did not go alone to Martinique. A young painter named Charles Laval accompanied him as an enthusiastic adherent of his idea of the simple decorative structure of painting. The life Gauguin had led for the last few years had made great inroads on his powerful constitution. Having never been used to frugality, his mode of living in straitened circumstances became extremely irregular. One day he would be starving, and another, if he got a little money, he would have a violent craving to enjoy the good things he had been forced to deny himself; and in his depressed condition he often went farther than was good for his health. In tobacco and alcohol, especially brandy, he very often found dangerous allies in deadening the gloom that stole over him in the hours of darkness. He had every reason to rely on his iron constitution, but this confidence was often somewhat exaggerated, so that when at last he fell ill he was apt to treat it lightly.

Both he and Laval, who was a naturally delicate man, were very soon affected by the tropical climate, and Gauguin, as the stronger, had in the first place to attend to his sick friend, until he was able to get him sent back to France as a doomed man. And both

the scenery and the people disappointed Gauguin; civilization had set its mark on them. The primitive nakedness he had expected to find had lost its natural charm; European civilization had dressed up the natives in clothes that made them appear frivolous. But the pictures he was able to paint in Martinique did satisfy to some extent his longing to encounter the simple and primitive. He was strongly impelled to pursue his aim and his basic idea was made clearer and simpler. If he had not yet got a grip of the leading motive, he had felt the underlying idea and the rhythm that was to accompany and support it. This had given him fresh courage and fresh impulses, and thereby his self-confidence was further invigorated to resume the struggle for his idea of depicting life in its nakedness, stripped of the atmosphere with which the age surrounds it. With his strong sexual instinct it was the primeval force in life itself that he was in quest of. But the climate and tropical disease broke down his health, and he could establish no intimacy with the inhabitants of the island. Solitude oppressed him.

He seized the first opportunity of returning to France as a seaman aboard a sailing-ship. He was ill, but his vision of the work he meant to produce was clearer than before. He had painted a score of pictures and wanted to show them to somebody. If they did not understand it all, they must at any rate grasp

something. He was in need of friendly care and some-one to talk to, and moreover he had not a penny in his pocket when after a long and exhausting voyage he reached Paris. There was only one place he could go — to Schuffenecker's.

Now that he was back in his native city, he could not help reflecting how strangely his life had turned out. Fifteen years before, he had arrived here poor and homeless, after having spent five years without any clear consciousness of what was his aim in life. A home was no reality, only an airy structure of memories and moods and a far-away romance in which his handsome and affectionate mother was the one he understood best, though she was mysterious as a woman. In the course of ten years he had made himself a home which was a reality. A good, well-managed house, with a woman he knew and loved, children he was proud and fond of, and a position he had made for himself without difficulty or struggle. He was respected and could afford to indulge his taste for art as an interested spectator, since he was making plenty of money without having to sell any-thing. And now he was back where he was fifteen years before, homeless and in need, after five years of vigorous development with a real aim before him and a full consciousness of its value for the future. And home was a reality, good and comfortable, but so far out of reach today. He was actually homeless

and more lonely than before, since he was no longer willing to be the Gauguin to whom doors were readily opened.

The only people he would go to now were Schuffenecker and his wife. With them he had been at home in a way before he had a home of his own. He had come to understand that their friendship was more deeply rooted than their respect for him as a prosperous citizen. He knew in his own mind that the misfortunes and bitter experiences of the last few years had not made him gentler or easier to get on with, that the gall had got into his blood to some extent. He was ill and wanted nursing, and suspected that some forbearance might be required, a thing for which he was not in the habit of asking.

Schuffenecker was now living in a little house with a studio, surrounded by a little garden, in the rue Boulard. Small as the place was, these excellent people found room for their friend, at whose disposal the studio was placed. The very next day Gauguin filled it with his pictures, putting a fresh canvas on his easel, and his host was delighted and full of admiration for his recent works from Martinique.

Schuffenecker himself was of no great account as an artist and therefore went very cautiously to work in the execution of his own pictures, but at the same time he attached importance to anything that might appear new and original. For this reason, like the

small circle of younger painters who were starting the Post-Impressionist school, he was ardently enthusiastic over Pissarro's ideas of the division of colour into the primitive colours of the spectrum carried out with oblique strokes of the brush, but without understanding their consequences or considering their importance. Apart from Seurat and Signac, whose personal views of the system led them to take a line of their own and to carry out their individual scheme, the rest of the Post-Impressionists were ready to snatch at any synthesis if only it appeared original and rebellious. And Schuffenecker followed it up, groping his way, and held forth about it with an eloquence and a generosity which carried many along with him who were less cautious without being much more richly endowed than he. With all his enthusiasm for art he was a modest painter who was aware of his own limitations. And perhaps his modesty prevented his seeing the limitations of others. Gauguin, who himself had a very good eye for other men's work and was a very good judge of it, relying more on the characteristics each personality put into his painting than on the external artistic form, did not view any syntheses with favour, least of all those that had to do with Symbolism. But Schuffenecker looked upon Gauguin as a genius, and his recent pictures entirely convinced him of it. The acts of a genius were not to be reconciled with common sense,

and of no one was this more true than of Gauguin; at any rate his actions were not normal, but they had their own profound significance, which found expression in his pictures and was not to be comprehended by ordinary mortals except in periphrasis.

To him Gauguin became something like a sacred animal that he had to exhibit, whose art he had to explain and translate. He would get quite excited, forget himself, interrupt and contradict his genius, when the latter coolly, laconically, and without exaggeration either of persuasiveness or affability explained his painting to all the artists and connoisseurs Schuffenecker brought to his studio. Occasionally he forgot Gauguin altogether, when the latter, feeling tired, had withdrawn into a corner behind the easel to mope over a brandy with a cigarette in his mouth.

And one day when Schuffenecker came with Theo van Gogh in tow — brother of Vincent and employed by Goupil, the art dealer — Gauguin forgot his host, shut the door of his own studio in his face, and turned the key. Not till next day, after many entreaties and assurances, in which the wife and the two daughters took part, was the door opened again.

For the kind-hearted Schuffenecker, who had only acted rather precipitately from pure unselfishness, there was no difficulty in offering apologies. To Gauguin that was impossible. Pardoning others may be an easy matter, pardoning oneself is more difficult. All he could do was to assure them that his friendly

feelings were unaltered. But he had to move, in order
to compose himself and settle down to his art.

While still staying with his friends in the rue
Boulard, Gauguin had taken up ceramics. This enabled him to combine form and colour in a natural
way, and at the Musée Guimet he found models in
primitive pottery which at the same time satisfied
his craving for simplicity. Most of his productions
he signed with a simple " P. Go." in place of the
elaborate and ornamental " Paul Gauguin " with
which he had previously furnished his pictures. But
this work kept him in Paris, though he was again
longing to get away. He rented a little studio with
money Theo van Gogh had furnished as an advance
on pictures he had deposited with the dealer after a
little exhibition. Once more hope was dawning and
with it the longing to find the motive which might
restore his full energy and enable him to overcome
the malady, both mental and physical, which constantly tormented him. And now his thoughts turned
again to the bold and simple scenery of Brittany and
its people, who seem carved out of the very landscape. A letter from Vincent van Gogh describing
Arles and the Arlésiennes in simple and picturesque
terms made him hesitate for a moment, since he was
also strongly attracted by this man in whom the yet
unimpaired beauty of the primitive was united with
a receptive and at the same time brilliant and independent spirit. But he decided on Brittany, not feel-

ing strong enough as yet for a calm encounter with
the magnetism of van Gogh's strong and decided
personality.

When the mild weather had definitely set in after
the hard winter, he moved to Pont-Aven in order to
prepare himself for a new spell of work as soon as
the frost was thawed out of his spirit and spring
had asserted itself in the storm-swept landscape of
Brittany.

" *Dear Mette,*

" I have just received the underclothes you sent
me; thanks, they fit very well and I was badly in
want of them. Since I came here I have been in bed
nearly all the time: I had to resort to a blister on the
liver. I can't manage to get rid of all the bile that
accumulates there.

" You tell me in your letter that you find it very
difficult to write in the state of mind which you are
in. I can understand its being painful to write me
your gossip; do something simpler. Send me, every
three weeks or so, just a word: *The children and I
are well.*

" They have discovered a new *remedy for head-
ache: antipyrin;* I assure you it is an excellent cure
and you ought to use it. You complain of being alone
and you tell me to remember you. I don't quite understand; you have your children about you, your
compatriots, your sisters and your brothers, your

LANDSCAPE
BRITTANY, 1888

LANDSCAPE

home. What am I to say of myself, alone in the bedroom of an inn, absolute silence from morning to
night? Nobody with whom I could exchange an
idea. Assuming that we were in a position to live as
in old days, you would complain at the end of a week
— but we haven't got so far. I believe I shall be able
to help you liberally in a year's time and I shall do
so as soon as I can. But as to sharing a home again,
I don't see any possibility of that for seven or eight
years. Let us hope that I shall then find a compensa-
tion for my domestic worries in the pleasure my children will give me. Being old, both of us, *we* shall
perhaps be able to understand each other better.
Cheer up and let us wait.

" Kiss the children for me.

" *Paul Gauguin* "

In Brittany Gauguin lodged with Madame Gloanec, who kept a boarding-house much frequented
by artists. But these were for the most part men who
were treading the old paths in their art — the thing
that he feared and despised above all. At first therefore he simply worked without seeking the society of
the others, until one day a few of Schuffenecker's
young friends arrived, among them Sérusier and
Émile Bernard, who aimed at following Gauguin on
his new and yet unblazed trail. And he was glad to
encourage them, because they gave him a stimulus
to intensive work in order to elucidate in his painting

the ideas he propounded to them. He was fully aware, however, that any impulses he gave them would quickly crumble away when they were left to themselves. Their admiration warmed him slightly, but he received little of the kind of encouragement he most needed, that which consisted in a personal comprehension of the true values in his own art. What he wanted was an independent spirit whose work was based on the same motives as his own, thus enabling him to measure his own strength. He was still haunted by the thought of his association with Vincent van Gogh; so he wrote to him and urged him to come to Pont-Aven. But van Gogh was too much attached to his beloved sunny Arles and asked Gauguin again to come there. He saw that Gauguin had need of him and had a feeling that he himself would benefit by the other's presence. He not only wrote to Gauguin, but also applied to his brother to help him:

" I write in all haste to tell you I have had a letter from Gauguin saying that he has not written to me before as he has been working hard. He says he is still ready to come south as soon as he has a chance.

" In the hope of sharing a studio with Gauguin I am going to decorate it. Nothing but sunflowers. The whole thing is to be a symphony in blue and yellow."

And van Gogh became more and more assiduous in his solicitude for his friend:

" I have had another letter from Gauguin. He

says he still has stomach trouble and he sounds depressed. He talks of being able to get hold of a capital of six hundred thousand francs to start an art dealer's business for the Impressionists. He wants to explain his scheme and says you are to be at the head of the affair. I shouldn't be surprised if this hope of his was a fata morgana, a mirage brought on by poverty. The deeper one sinks in poverty, especially if one is ill, the more one thinks of such possibilities. So this plan looks to me like a sign that he is getting frozen in and the best thing we can do is to get him moved as quickly as possible.

" I wonder whether he isn't quite ready to come here, only hotel and travelling expenses have been complicated by a doctor's bill. In other words, he finds it difficult. I think he ought to let his debts look after themselves and pawn his pictures. I had to do the same to get to Paris. Gauguin shall get enough to eat, he can take walks with me in this beautiful country, see what the house is like and how we can arrange it, and amuse himself as much as he likes. He has been living on short commons and it has made him ill, so that he can't tell a sad note from a merry one. It is high time he came and he will soon get well here. Meanwhile forgive me if I exceed my budget; I will work all the harder."

Van Gogh was full of impulsive geniality and high spirits, beaming with delight over trifles — a studio, a little house, and the prospect of having his friend to

look after made him happy and kept him busy. A
little irregularity and a difficulty about the rent never
made any impression on him. How different from
Gauguin, the optimist, who was always immersed
in great plans, who could not be kind without being
generous, could never stop at small sums, but must
always open his purse-strings wide — silent and
thorough when he had an account to settle!

Gauguin allowed himself to be persuaded and
went to Arles in August. At their first meeting the
two men had stimulated each other by an exchange
of artistic points of view, and this had encouraged
them both to work with renewed vigour. Now they
were to meet at a moment when both were in full
and rapid development; they were to work together,
to be each other's whetstone, strong and independent
personalities both of them, and so different. A dangerous experiment. And Gauguin had an instinctive
presentiment of this. But he had set his heart on it
and overcame his scruples.

" I arrived at Arles towards morning and waited
for dawn in a little night café. The proprietor looked
at me and exclaimed: ' You're the chum, I recognize
you.' A portrait of myself that I had sent to Vincent
is enough to explain this exclamation. Vincent had
shown him the portrait, telling him it was a chum
who was coming shortly.

" Not too early nor too late, I went and turned
Vincent out. The day was taken up with settling me

in my new quarters, with a lot of chatting and a walk, to give me a chance of sharing his admiration for the beauty of Arles and of the Arlésiennes, about whom, in parenthesis, I wasn't able to show much enthusiasm. Next day we were hard at work. . . .

" It took me a few weeks to reconcile myself entirely to the sharp taste of Arles and its neighbourhood. But that did not prevent our working hard; especially Vincent. Between our two natures, the one a regular volcano, the other boiling too, it looked as if a sort of struggle was in preparation.

" In the first place I found an untidiness everywhere which offended my eye. His colour-box was hardly big enough for all his squeezed tubes and it was never closed; but in spite of all this disorder, all this mess, his canvas shone with a glorious unity. There was the same confusion in his talk. Daudet, de Goncourt, and the Bible were afire in this Dutch brain. At Arles everything — the quays, the bridges, the boats, the whole Midi — had taken the place of Holland in his mind. He even forgot how to write Dutch and, as will be seen from his letters to his brother, he wrote an admirable French. In spite of all my efforts to deduce a logical reasoning in his critical opinions from this mental confusion, I could not find an explanation of all the contradictions between his painting and his views. Thus he had an unbounded admiration for Meissonier and a profound hatred of Ingres. Degas reduced him to de-

spair and Cézanne was only a bluffer. The thought of Monticelli made him weep.

" One thing that annoyed him was having to admit that I possessed a good deal of intelligence, while my forehead was low, a sign of fatuity. And with all this there went an immeasurable tenderness, or rather an altruism worthy of an apostle.

" In the course of a month I found the same traces of disorder in our common exchequer. What was I to do? The situation was critical. Our funds received, on his side, a modest contribution from his brother, who was employed at Goupil's; on my side, from a kind of bartering with pictures. It was necessary to speak out, but there was a danger of hurting his exaggerated sensitiveness.

" In order to solve the problem I had to proceed with the greatest caution and with an ingratiating air that was ill suited to my nature. I must admit that this was much more successful than I had anticipated."

Not only did Gauguin put their domestic affairs in order, he also took the lead in the feverish race of work in which both artists were very soon involved. He was inspired to do so by his affection for van Gogh's simple and primitive good nature and by his admiration for his intuitive original gifts. But unfortunately he did not guess that disease was already lurking in van Gogh's mind and that it was responsible for the sudden fits of suspicion which were so

entirely foreign to the man's nature. At such moments Gauguin's direct way of tackling things and his curt and blunt manner of asserting his opinions were apt to irritate the usually kind and indulgent van Gogh, with the clear, childlike eyes, whose joy it was to see his friend reviving and regaining his whole strength in a short time.

" How long were we together? I can't say — have forgotten. In spite of the suddenness of the catastrophe, in spite of the fever of work that had hold of me, this time seems to me a century. Though no one had a suspicion of it, here were two men performing a colossal task, useful to them both. Perhaps to others as well? Some things there are that bear fruit.

" When I came to Arles, Vincent was caught up in the Post-Impressionist school and it had brought him to a serious deadlock. Not because this school was a bad one, like all schools, but because it was not suited to his impatient and independent nature.

" With all this yellow against violet, all this work in the complementary colours, which as far as he was concerned was without plan, he only achieved weak, imperfect, and monotonous harmonies. They lacked the fanfare. I set myself the task of putting this straight, which I found easy, as I had a rich and fertile soil to work in. Like all original natures bearing the stamp of personality, Vincent was not afraid of his neighbour, nor was he obstinate. From that time

on, my van Gogh made astonishing progress; he now divined what was in him, the whole range of light in full sunshine. . . .

" I tell you this to let you see that van Gogh, without losing a scrap of his originality, profited by my teaching. And he was grateful for it every day. This is what he means when he writes to Albert Aurier that he owes much to Gauguin.

" When I came to Arles, van Gogh was still in the experimental stage, while I, a much older man, had taken final shape. I owe something to Vincent, and that is, in the knowledge of having been useful to him, the confirmation of my earlier ideas about painting; and then the being able to remind myself in moments of difficulty that there are other people more unhappy than myself. . . .

" During the latter part of my stay van Gogh was subject to sudden fits of temper, after which he would be silent. On some nights I surprised him as he was approaching my bed. How was it that I chanced to wake just then? I only had to say in a serious voice: ' What's wrong with you, Vincent? ' and without a word he would go back to bed and fall into a heavy sleep.

" I had taken it into my head to paint his portrait as he sat painting his favourite motive, sunflowers. When the picture was finished he said to me: ' Yes, that's me all right, but it's me gone mad.'

" That same evening we went to a café. He took

a weak absinthe. All of a sudden he threw the glass and its contents straight in my face. I dodged it, caught him round the waist, and went out of the café, across the place Victor Hugo. A few minutes later Vincent was in his bed; he fell asleep at once and did not wake till morning.

" On waking he said to me quite calmly: ' My dear Gauguin, I have a vague feeling that I insulted you last night.'

" ' I forgive you with all my heart; but yesterday's scene may be repeated, and if I am hit I may not be able to control myself and then I shall strangle you. So let me write to your brother to tell him I am returning.'

" My God, what a day!

" In the evening, after dinner, I felt I must go for a walk by myself and get some fresh air in the scent of flowering laurels. I had almost crossed the place Victor Hugo when I heard well-known steps behind me — short and rapid. I turned just as Vincent was rushing at me with an open razor in his hand.

" My glance must have been formidable, for he stopped and ran off home ashamed of himself. Was I cowardly at that moment; ought I not to have disarmed him and calmed him? I have often questioned my conscience, but without finding anything with which to reproach myself. Let him who will throw the first stone. I made for a hotel as fast as I could,

where, after asking the time, I got a room and went to bed. In my excitement I could not get to sleep till about three in the morning and woke up fairly late, about half past seven. When I reached our house I saw a crowd of people. In front of the house were some gendarmes and a little man in a derby hat, the police superintendent.

" What had happened? Van Gogh had come home and had at once cut off his ear close to the head. It had taken him a good while to stop the bleeding, for next day there were towels soaked in blood spread out on the floor below, and the two rooms and the stairs leading to our bedroom were stained with blood.

" As soon as he was fit to go out, with his head completely enveloped in a béret, he had made for a house where, failing a sweetheart, one can be supplied with an acquaintance, and had given the concierge his ear, neatly wrapped and enclosed in an envelope. ' Here's a souvenir of me.' After that he went quickly home; went to bed and slept. He took care nevertheless to close the shutters and place a lighted lamp on a table near the window. Ten minutes later the whole street allotted to the prostitutes had heard the story and everybody was talking about it.

" I hadn't a notion of all this when I reached our door, where the man in the derby addressed me brutally in a tone that was more than brusque: ' What

have you done with your friend? ' — ' I don't know.'
— ' Oh yes, you know well enough — he's dead.'

" I don't wish anybody a moment like that and it
took me some time to gather my thoughts and let my
heart settle down. I was overwhelmed with anger,
indignation, sorrow, besides the feeling of shame at
all these eyes ransacking my person, and I stammered
out: ' Well, monsieur, let us go in; we can have our
explanation indoors.'

" Vincent lay doubled up in bed with the sheets
rolled round him. He looked like a dead man. Cautiously, very gently, I touched his body and felt the
warmth which told me he was alive. And then all
my wits and my energy came back to me. Almost in
a whisper I said to the police superintendent: ' Wake
this man with every possible care, and if he asks
after me tell him I have gone to Paris. The sight
of me might be fatal.' I must admit that from this
moment the police were as obliging as could be, and
had the sense to send for a cab and a doctor.

" On waking, Vincent asked for his friend, his
pipe, and his tobacco, and even thought of the cash-
box containing our money. Suspicion, no doubt! But
it made no impression on me; I was already impervi-
ous to suffering. Vincent was taken at once to the
hospital, and there his brain gave out altogether.

" What happened afterwards is known to all who
are interested in it and there is no need to touch upon
anything but the infinite suffering of a man who was

being treated in a madhouse and at intervals of some months recovered his reason sufficiently to understand his condition and to work feverishly at painting the most extraordinary pictures we know.

" His last letter is from Auvers near Pontoise. He says he had hoped to recover sufficiently to be able to visit me in Brittany, but now he was obliged to face the fact that a cure was impossible. ' *Cher Maître* ' (the only time he used this expression), ' when one has known you and caused you pain it is fitter to die in possession of one's senses than in a state that is merely degrading.'

" He put a bullet into his stomach and died a few hours later, lying in his bed and smoking his pipe, with his mind perfectly clear, full of his art and with no hatred for anyone. In *Les Monstres* Jean Dolent writes: ' When Gauguin utters the name Vincent, his voice softens.' Without knowing, he has guessed it; Dolent is right. We know why."

In reality van Gogh's fate made a very deep impression on Gauguin. When alone with his thoughts, he would often work himself up till he burst into tears, and at times he even addressed an absent person earnestly and tenderly, but when faced by anything that appealed to his feelings, he was shy and afraid of giving himself away. He took refuge behind a mask, which may have concealed a violent emotion, but had more the appearance of arrogance. He was unwilling to speak of those events in his life which

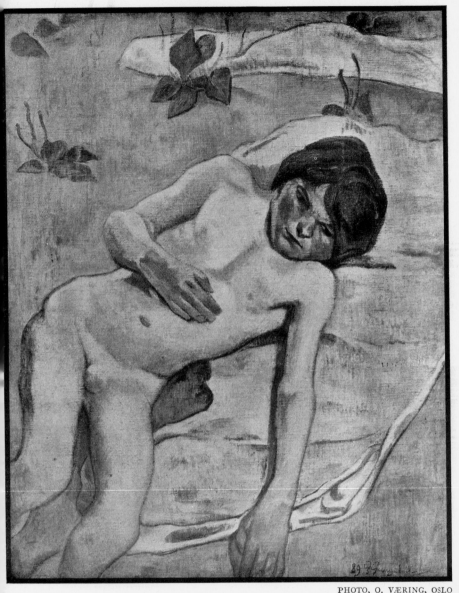

NUDE
BRITTANY, 1889

LANDSCAPE

had made a strong impression on him, particularly where an explanation or excuse for his conduct might have been called for. This silence was often interpreted as indifference. He knew that this was so and it made him persist in his silence, even when someone tried to relieve the painful situation which often arose. And so it was with his association with van Gogh; with a throbbing heart and a wounded spirit his reserve only increased the coldness around him.

He did not stay long in Paris. He went back to Brittany, but not to Pont-Aven. He chose Le Pouldu, a little fishing-village hidden away among pleasant hills, but nearer the sea than Pont-Aven and more secluded.

He had to get away from civilization, with all the complicated forms it insists upon before allowing one to develop freely and naturally. The views and customs of the time are imposed upon one, and it was precisely against these that his natural disposition was often in revolt. He wanted to escape from the narrow limits Christian society sets for what it calls the normal, whether in its view of life or the expression the artist finds for it. And yet — he was haunted by the longing for his family, that tragic longing which made him constantly think of his position in society.

" An artist's duty is to work in order to grow strong; I have done this, and everything I have brought home meets with nothing but admiration.

And yet I don't get on. . . . But even if it is very difficult, there is a chance that one day I shall occupy the place I deserve. To whom will you then apply, and will your advisers, who are not your paymasters, still tell you that your existence is not bound up with that of your husband? "

" A day will come when *your* children will be able to present themselves to anybody, no matter where, under their father's name in order to obtain advancement and honour. At twenty the boys will have to make a position for themselves. Do you suppose the powerful friends I shall then have made will not be ready to help them? And I don't believe I should have achieved this as a business man."

" You know me: I either calculate (and I'm good at figures) or I do *not* calculate; and then I fight with bared chest, eyes front.

" Very well, I accept the part allotted to me. That being so, I must *calculate* not to drop the substance for the shadow. And the shadow is the position of an employee. I should have a salary of 2,000 or 4,000 francs, what your brothers are getting, and then what could I be reproached with? Nothing. And yet we should both be in much the same position. As to the future, nobody thinks of that.

" In spite of the assurance of my conscience I have not failed to consult others (men of some account) to find out if I was doing my duty. They all agreed with me, that my business is art, it is my capital, it is the

future of my children, it is the honour of the name I have given them — all things which will serve them one day. Therefore I work at my art, which is nothing (in money) for the moment (times are bad), but which will take shape in the future. That is a long time to wait, you will say, but what do you expect me to do about it, is it my fault? And I am the chief sufferer. I can assure you that if the people who know had said that I had no talent and was lazy, I should have given up long ago. Can one say that Millet failed in his duty and abandoned his children to a miserable future?

" I have told you that my intention is to see my children, but that I will not venture to go out with them, miserably dressed as I am now."

These tragical alternatives were constantly struggling in Paul Gauguin's mind, and the existence he led intensified the struggle. It was one of hope and disappointment, freedom and duty, riches or poverty. For him there was no middle course, no golden mean. And this was what put him at odds with society, where mediocrity is normal. And mediocrity judges those who stand outside from two quite opposite points of view. They are looked upon either as geniuses or as imbeciles.

It was not long before Gauguin was surrounded by a band of young artists, who were ready to worship the master and his ideas — and to build up a school on them, a thing which he found entirely aim-

less. But it gave him a feeling that he did not stand quite alone in his art; it even gave him a foretaste of the fame which in spite of his craving for the primitive he still regarded as his future aim.

In many ways Le Pouldu and its inhabitants supplied a frame for the primitive and romantic; the place had grown up in centuries of local and simple traditions, and fitted naturally into the scenery, which with its undulating forms and wind-swept vegetation gave it shelter from the sea and its capricious changes of weather. And the inhabitants were angular people with boldly cut features, whose expression bore the stamp of their religious ideas, a blend of Christianity and pagan superstition, in which the deity was rather the just but cruel judge who demands human life than the white, gentle Christ who promises eternal life.

The painted crucifix at the crossways outside the town was both comforter and avenger.

In the little inn Gauguin and his young friends used to meet, and it was not long before its bar parlour was converted into a sort of temple in a grotesque and nondescript style and the windows were decorated in bright colours. All the woodwork was carved, and among foliage, human and animal forms text-like sentences were interwoven, such as *Soyez amoureuses et vous serez heureuses,* or *Soyez mystérieuses.* Gauguin presided over the little circle that assembled here at dusk after an industrious day. His

LE CHRIST JAUNE

BRITTANY, 1889

BONJOUR, MONSIEUR GAUGUIN
BRITTANY, 1889

longish hair under the béret — worn aslant and well over the forehead — formed a dark frame for the powerful, weather-beaten face, making it shine in the half-light. A rough suit of rustic cut with carved buttons; underneath, a knitted jersey in a bold Breton pattern, and over all a loose cloak held together at the throat by a gilt chain. All this gave him a singular appearance; a pair of big sabots carved and painted in barbaric colours completed the picture, in which the rather small and elegant but powerful hands offered the only striking contrast. Everything about him was strongly marked and calculated rather to keep people at a distance than to draw them nearer.

It was as though Gauguin wished to insist that his art must not be expected to conform to the normal. But there was a certain consistent harmony in his attire, which together with his personality announced that the type of beauty he aimed at was not based on current principles.

It was in Brittany and especially in the year 1889 that Gauguin's artistic form took definite shape. It laid stress on the decorative side both in composition and in colour and depended in a very remarkable degree on strong and simple effects in the treatment of the material and in the colour impression; but at the same time he aimed at plastic form both in figures and landscape and achieved this more by his drawing than by modelling with the help of light and shade. The model and the landscape were quite

necessary to him, but he took no account of the instantaneous impression; each thing had to have its purpose in the decorative whole, and yet each must also express a plastic feeling in virtue of its original characteristics. Beauty did not consist in the happy chance the artist had lighted upon; it was the character of each object and its purely physical expression that Gauguin brought together in a harmonious whole in order to create beauty. To him colour composition, the colouristic element, was not so much the combination which produces the effects of light and shade, proximity and distance, as a powerful expression of temperamental oscillations in the mind on receiving impressions from outside. And yet his instinct for nature was so strong and he himself was so near to reality that he hated to hear the word " synthesis " and it gave him a cold sweat to be taken symbolically. Without laying down a definite program he foreshadowed Expressionism in his painting and thus found himself in the strongest opposition to the Impressionists, who were now becoming more and more fashionable in the galleries of the modern picture dealers.

When winter was drawing on, Gauguin went back to Paris in order if possible to improve his financial position; he was now well supplied with pictures and it seemed as though attention was beginning to be centred on him in certain quarters. He stayed at Schuffenecker's again for a short time, but as soon

as he had a little money he moved to a room in the rue Delambre and was accommodated in the studio of a painter named Daniel de Monfreid, whose acquaintance he had made at Schuffenecker's. " The Captain," as Monfreid was called by his intimates, was a man of ardent activity and varied talents, which he turned to account in a small way, now as the skipper of a small craft in which he made trips all over the Mediterranean, now as a painter, and now as a farmer on an estate he owned in the Pyrenees. He was well enough off to be able to pursue his different avocations without having to think of daily bread, and without such pretensions as might urge him to aim high. He was a practical man and knew how to adapt his life to his conditions and capabilities. It therefore gave him a special pleasure to straighten things out for other, less practical men when his accurate judgment of artistic values led him to regard them as possessed of qualities as yet undiscovered. With all his modesty and simplicity he had a respect for fame and loved to be in its vicinity, even when it overshadowed him. It might even be said that he was a little jealous of others who approached too close to a celebrity he regarded as his own property.

In a purely personal way he did not feel particularly attracted to Gauguin, but he scented the great artist. He himself had great outward cordiality of manner and a lively interest in everything and every-

body. Gauguin's reserved and taciturn nature and his apparent self-absorption made de Monfreid chary of being drawn into too intimate relations with him.

" Gauguin was a great artist and I admired and loved him as such, and helped him, too, to the best of my ability; but I am glad I was never very closely connected with him personally."

Gauguin did not have to be very long in Paris before discovering that his working powers were giving out. In Brittany he had missed the nude model, the grown-up Bretonne being extremely reluctant to expose her nudity; but the Parisian model, whose figure and gestures were adapted to a refined external elegance, afforded him no inspiration. In addition to this he was distracted by his surroundings, and the strong contrast of light and shade when working indoors called for a method entirely opposed to that which he aimed at. To be between four walls was to him like being in a prison cell, and the room he lived in, with its bed, table, chair, and wash-stand, was quite in that style.

If he stayed in Paris it was in order to meet fresh people with whom he could discuss his artistic ideas and because he still hoped that some day a door might open, leading to better financial prospects.

At the Café Voltaire in the place de l'Odéon a number of literary men with new ideas used to meet in the evening, and Gauguin joined them. Here sat Verlaine, broken down and ill; Charles Morice eagerly

championing the young Symbolist movement; Jean
Moréas and Albert Aurier listening with critical interest. And here came Rodin and Carrière, who
with his brilliant appraisement of art was very soon
acutely interested in Gauguin's exposition of his artistic views, so entirely opposed to his own. Occasionally an intimate little banquet was held at the café,
which helped the habitués to know each other better.

" A long table. On each side, plates and glasses are
laid in a straight line, so that the effect of the perspective is to make the table long, very long. This is
a banquet. Stéphane Mallarmé is in the chair. Opposite him sits Jean Moréas, the Symbolist. The guests
are Symbolists. Perhaps the waiters are too. Right at
the end of the table is Clovis Hugues (Marseilles).
Far away at the other end is Barrès (Paris).

" We dine; there are toasts. The chairman speaks
first; Moréas replies. Clovis Hugues, plethoric,
long-haired, and highfalutin, makes a long speech,
of course in verse. Barrès, tall, thin, and bald, quotes
Baudelaire, dryly and in prose. We listen. The marble gives one a chill. My neighbour, who is a young
man, but fat, with gorgeous diamonds sparkling in
the thousand pleats of his shirt-front, asks me in a
whisper: ' Is Monsieur Baudelaire here this evening? ' I scratch my knee: ' Yes, he's sitting down
there, and, by the way, it's about him Barrès is talking.' — ' Oh, I should like so much to be introduced
to him.'

" Somewhere or other a saint says to his penitents: ' Beware of the pride of humility.' "

In a circle like this Gauguin came to life and became more communicative. These writers stimulated his intellect, since each of them had a place in his own range of ideas, a circumstance which not infrequently spurred him to contradiction. But these men also judged his views by the light of their own without taking up his ideas and following them out. And they listened to what he had to say, and evidently received reciprocal inspiration from him. Noticing this he became persuaded that one day his work too must be capable of exciting interest, and perhaps in a not too distant future. But if the evenings at the Café Voltaire diverted him, café life in many ways enhanced his feeling of solitude and homelessness and at the same time told upon his strength, for during these talks frequent recourse was had to brandy and cigarettes without much attention being paid to it at the time by himself or others. When he awoke after a brief and heavy sleep in a cold, dark room all his misfortunes and responsibilities came stealing over him, accompanied by longing for his home and the bitter feeling of solitude. His thoughts tore at him till his heart throbbed with fear and he longed for daylight, dreading to doze off and be assailed by nightmares. And with the day began the struggle with that cursed heart which could only be stilled by the bottle, in company which obliged

LANDSCAPE
BRITTANY, 1889

YOUNG WOMAN

him to conceal his unrest and brought him calm.

He let things drift during the winter months, when he could not work anyway; but spring was approaching and some change had to be made.

One day Gauguin made up his mind to visit Copenhagen and see his children. And, once the decision had been made, his old inflexible resolution returned. He raised money for the journey, enough for a stay at a good hotel. His wardrobe was completed with a pair of shoes and a new béret; otherwise it had to be content with pressing. Then he wrote to say he was coming. At the station in Copenhagen he was received by his wife and the two eldest children, Émile and Aline. His outlandish appearance was reflected in their looks. The long hair and a slight tendency to corpulence had changed their recollection of him. And he himself was astonished to find how different the image he had preserved of his family was from the reality. Mette had cut her hair quite short, and the two ingenuous childish figures had now become lanky adolescents who greeted him with awkward hesitation in clumsy French. Mette chaffed him about his altered appearance, and this brought some relief and led to practical discussions. Arm in arm with the two children he was able quietly to gain their confidence.

His stay in Copenhagen was not of long duration, nor did the prevailing atmosphere encourage it. Many conflicting emotions were at work in Mette's

mind. Her image of the husband she had been fond
of had changed even during the last two years of
their life together, and although during their sepa-
ration it had recovered something of its former attraction, causing her to miss him in her loneliness,
he was now so altered that her apprehensions about
resuming their life in common entirely overcame
the cordiality she would have liked to show him,
since she pitied him as much as she pitied herself.
Being more practical than amatory, she did not let
her feelings run away with her, but reviewed all the
consequences this might entail. She came to the conclusion that, things being as they were, he too would
be best served by her acting as she did and had done.
She took her stand on the present, where he thought
of the future.

With Gauguin's powerfully erotic nature the
meeting with Mette had revived his love for her, so
that he interpreted her attitude as treachery to him,
planned by her correct and unimaginative family,
which placed duty before feelings. But he felt sure
of being able to overcome this resistance in time, and
this contributed to make him still more strongly attached to his family. Not only had his sense of duty
been roused, but also his instinct as the husband of
the woman he had loved and who had to be recon-
quered. But the strongest bond was that which bound
him to the two eldest children, especially Aline. The
three younger ones were too small to interest him,

and, as things were, their childish shyness made them doubly strange to him. But his daily intercourse with the two eldest brought back memories and loosened the tongues of all three, giving him an insight into their minds, where he found a tenderness he had so sorely missed and longed to be able to express in the life he had been leading. With them he could be what he was in his art; simply and naturally he could touch the chords of tenderness in living human children. They were his and he saw much of himself in them, especially in Aline, who bore a strong outward resemblance to him, and whose disposition oscillated between violent emotion and shy reserve. She was the one who best understood the happiness of having her father with them, as she had missed him most and had also felt ashamed when asked who and where her father was, the father whose name was always mentioned with a certain awkwardness in the family circle.

What a joy it was to these children when in the mild April weather they drove in an open carriage through the streets and people turned to look at the queer foreigner who sat leaning back between his two children, Émile proud and cheerful in his schoolboy's uniform, Aline stirred and happy! Many a tangled perplexity was smoothed out in Gauguin's mind in the three weeks during which he laid it open to his children.

CHAPTER 5

GAUGUIN was disinclined to talk about the realities of his sailor days; the actual life on board ship had left no impressions beyond those of coarseness and fisticuffs, which were not to his taste. Although he was a good boxer, strong and lithe, he had no disposition for contests of strength. But the dream of a voyage to parts unknown, the fleeting memories of a wild shore-leave, had left their marks and constantly recurred to him. In his long sleepless nights he read books of travel, Pierre Loti, Élisée Reclus, and in particular *Le Journal des Voyages*. His dreams of roving were still alive. They added to his restlessness and his desire to get away from a society in which he felt less and less at home and where he no longer found the inspiration for realizing his artistic ideal. Not yet had he quite found the formula for his painting; it still fell short of the greatest. And that was what he aimed at; he wished to be in the forefront of contemporary art and to reach the zenith of his own powers as artist and creator.

" If some day the clouds disperse, one should be able to bid defiance to oneself or to say: ' I haven't got it, but I shall get it.' And to go on like this until one is old."

The dream of roving grew in his mind and urged him to new voyages of discovery, and one day he determined that it should be realized, so that at last he might come home bringing his dream with him. The dream of the naked primitive beauty in nature. *Le Mariage de Loti* and a tempting official description of the glories of the South Sea Islands decided him for Tahiti.

" The day will come, and that soon, when I shall hide in the forests of the South Sea island to live in rapture, in peace, and in art, surrounded by a family, far from the European fight for money. There in Tahiti, in the beautiful nights of the tropics, I shall be able to listen to the gently murmuring music of my quivering heart in loving harmony with the mysterious beings that surround me. Free at last, without money cares, I shall be able to love, to sing, and to die."

He was still taking refuge in his dreams, but when his decision was made in earnest, his practical sense awoke and he returned to the realities of existence, but strong, active, and full of hope. All the worries, difficulties, and encumbrances of daily life became trifles compared with the prospect which now opened before him.

His mistress Juliette, who had only known him for the last three months, watched with surprise and misgiving the intense determination that had so suddenly possessed her otherwise introspective and low-spirited friend. All the preparations he was making pointed to a change, and his plans were made at the Café Voltaire. Thirty of his best pictures were to be sold at auction. He got Octave Mirbeau to write the introduction to the catalogue and shortly before the sale it was printed in the *Echo de Paris*, to which Mirbeau was a contributor. Through the intervention of people of influence Gauguin was given an official but unpaid post in Tahiti by the Director of the Fine Arts, Ary Renan, together with a promise to buy some of the pictures he would paint there. The auction itself was very well attended, everyone had been drummed up and his friends of the Café Voltaire applauded vigorously. The sale brought in 9,860 francs, and the highest price paid was 900 francs for the picture representing Jacob wrestling with the angel in the presence of a number of Bretonne women. Another picture, *La Belle Angèle*, a portrait of Madame Satre, the hostess of Pont-Aven, was bought by some friends and offered to her as a gift; but she declined it on account of the devastating criticism it met with from some of her more distinguished artist visitors.

On March 23rd a farewell party was held at the Café Voltaire, when Gauguin's health was drunk in

JACOB WRESTLING WITH THE ANGEL
1889

FROM LE POULDU
1890

Beaujolais after an improvised speech, full of feeling, from Jean Dolent; and this time Gauguin did not succeed in disguising his emotion: in a scarcely audible voice he was only able to stammer a laconic " Thanks! "

At last the future he had so long hoped for seemed to be approaching.

" *My adored Mette*,

" An adoration which often enough is full of bitterness. As you will see, our letters have crossed, and if this last letter has been delayed it is because I was waiting for the photographs — but anyhow let us not return letter for letter (I beseech you), but let us write what we have to write at the proper time. I know how difficult you must find the present time, but now the future is assured and I shall be happy — very happy, if you will share it with me.

" Failing passions, we shall be able — with white hair — to enter an era of peace and spiritual happiness, surrounded by our children, flesh of our flesh. As I have told you: your family is wrong to put you against me, but in spite of that I will not take any notice of them.

" Yesterday a dinner was given in my honour at which forty-five people were present, painters and authors, presided over by Mallarmé. Verses, toasts, and the warmest homage paid to me. I assure you that in three years' time I shall have made a success

that will permit us — you and I — to live untroubled by difficulties. You shall rest and I shall work.

" Perhaps one day it will dawn on you what sort of man you have made the father of your children. I am proud of my name and I will make it a great name, and I hope — nay, I am sure that you will not be the one to soil it — even if you should meet a dashing captain. If you go to Paris I will ask you to associate only with decent, straightforward people, and not charlatans.

" When you come let Morice know by letter beforehand, as he is a bachelor. He will at once assist you to meet decent people. The government has given me a formal mission, so that when I get there I shall have a call on the personnel of the Navy, the hospital, and so on. Furthermore I have had a commission for a picture, 3,000 francs, when I come back. All this will help to bring us together again. Good-bye, dear Mette, dear children, love me well. And when I come back we will be married again. So this is a betrothal kiss that I send you today.

" Your Paul "

Gauguin was too full of the successful way in which his wishes were being accomplished to notice the incongruity in conventional eyes between the bohemian life into which he had been forced by circumstances and the respectable future to which he

was looking forward. In spite of bitter experience he had not yet learned how strict and short-sighted are the laws of respectability and how unwilling they are to admit the truth that necessity is the mother of lawfulness in the natural instincts. Especially with strong and productive men whose creative ability calls on them to follow their nature without concealment or excuse. But society only forgives the penitent, or him who pays in cash.

Gauguin could neither repent nor pay; he had to pursue his object, guided by his nature and strong sexual instinct.

His parting with Juliette was not easy. Poor child, she knew that to her he would not come back; she would be left alone with the child she was expecting. All he had promised her was that if it was a daughter she should be called Marie, his mother's second name. He would not forget her.

At the beginning of April 1891 he boarded at Marseilles the boat which was to take him to his long-wished-for Tahiti. In the very first days his impatience piled up clouds on the horizon.

" *Dear Daniel,*

" Would you believe it, my voyage via Nouméa is likely to take a long time and to cost an additional 500 francs, as they tell me the connection is as irregular as it can be. It is quite likely (they tell me again) to take three to five months.

" So warn our friends: if any of them thinks of making the voyage let him take the direct route, New York–San Francisco, etc.

" It was stupid of me to take second class, third is almost as good and I should have saved 500 francs —

" Just a word in haste so as not to miss the mail. — Give Juliette a cordial kiss from me.

" Hearty greetings to all artist friends.

" *P. Go* "

But fortune seemed to smile on Gauguin. At Nouméa the boat lay ready to put to sea, out into the great Pacific towards his goal: the little South Sea Islands which look like innocent fly-spots on the map of the world. One would think these little islands had no importance, at least to European eyes, and might be left in peace — a reminder of paradise and of primitive, carefree barbarism, in contrast to the economic struggle which life has become in civilized countries.

" I am going to Tahiti, a little island in the ocean, where one can live one's material life without money. A terrible time is preparing for the next generation in Europe: the realm of gold. Everything is rotten, people and art. One is continually torn to pieces. Down there in any case the Tahitians have only to stretch out their hands to find food in a soil of wonderful fertility and beneath a sky that knows no winter."

But European and American skippers in their
voyages over the ocean have sought shelter and adventures on these idyllic islands, and on their recom-
mendation the governments have sent a cruiser and
planted their flag with an alarming salute of guns.
Thus is inaugurated the extermination, by the aid of
Christianity, European culture (in other words, fear
of nature's nakedness), and — syphilis, of a barbaric
and beautiful race, who are robbed of their patri-
mony for no better purpose than that it may serve as
a counter in an unimportant commercial treaty between two great powers. In a hundred years the traces
of this race will only be found in the ethnographical
museums of the great capitals, or will be studied as
primitive art — a blurred picture of a people whose
only characteristics were beauty and natural vitality.
As yet the ruins had not collapsed, the broken statue
still smiled amid a rich and luxuriant nature.

For these islands Gauguin was bound; his eye
scanned the horizon daily for a group, Tahiti, to appear above the infinite surface of the Pacific, where
all that was to be seen was the narrow streak of the
ship's wake and the string of porpoises.

Gauguin was familiar with the sea; the three
months' voyage had a calming effect on him. A
gentler mood came over him as he recalled the times
when as a youth he had stood as now, looking out for
land, and often it had been the coast of that land on
which he had just turned his back that he had then

longed to see. Now too, as he was carried farther and
farther from France until no more than its bare outline was visible, he had to admit to himself that, even
if his life had often been a hard one, it had been very
far from empty and was bound up with emotions and
events from which he could not entirely dissociate
himself, although something recalcitrant in his nature was constantly in revolt against them. His absorption in the greatness of European art became
clearer to him day by day; it was the standard by
which he would measure his own greatness; and then
the recalcitrant spirit returned, bidding him follow
nothing but his natural instincts. It was as though
there were two personalities within him which led
to continual conflict both in his life and in his art. On
the one side culture and education, the admiration of
technical skill and decorative beauty; on the other
the barbarian who was bent on following his primitive and natural instincts and discovering the naked
beauty in nature. Now that he believed he could
combine his dream of the manifestation of the primitive instincts with reality, he was encountering it
with the eyes of the European and with the tension
resulting from being free to be honest with his nature
without having to consider the moral laws established by the society to which he really belonged and
from which his pretensions did not permit him entirely to liberate himself. In his art he could show
that his dream possessed a beauty of its own. And at

the same time the dream, being translated into reality, might proclaim that the healthy and normal manifestations of life are those which have most influence on the course of life, and that therefore, regardless of other considerations, he must allow his own nature and instincts to be the fundamental motives in his art.

" I don't complain; I say in the words of Jesus: That which is born of the flesh is flesh, and that which is born of the Spirit is spirit. Thanks to this, I can satisfy my flesh for a few coppers, and my spirit is left in peace.

" Thus I am exhibited to the public as an animal bereft of any feeling and incapable of selling my soul for a pearl. I have not been a Werther and I don't intend to be a Faust. Who knows? Perhaps the infected and the alcoholic will be the men of the future. It looks to me as if morality, the sciences, and all the rest of it were heading for a new morality which possibly will be the opposite of that of today. Marriage, the family, and a whole lot of fine things that are dinned into my ears give me a distinct impression of flying off at full gallop. And then you ask me to agree with you.

" Coition is a serious matter.

" In matrimony the greater cuckold is the lover, as a Palais-Royal piece tells us: *The Luckiest of Three*.

" I had bought some photographs at Port Said of

the Fall of Man, taken in the very act. They were
hung quite openly in my bedroom. Men, women,
even children have been amused by them; pretty
nearly everybody was amused for a moment and
thought no more of it. Only those who call themselves respectable wouldn't come to see me, and they
think about it all the year round.

" Think it over and stick up something indecent
in full view over your door; then you'll get rid of the
respectable people, the most insufferable of God's
creatures."

So hard a shell had he grown; but the shell concealed forces both strong and tender which could
now be set free if only he could find a simple and
natural mode of life to nullify the effect that lack of
appreciation, together with strong personal conviction, had had upon a prolific and creative nature, but
one which was critical and exacting, restlessly seeking for a connection between logical reasoning and
strong emotion, between reality and illusion.

All this Gauguin hoped to find in the group of
islands which was now becoming visible on the
horizon.

" On the night of June 8th, after a voyage of
sixty-three days from place to place, days which for
me were full of impatient dreaming, of feverish
longing for the promised land, we caught sight of
some strange specks of light moving in zigzag fashion

on the sea. A black cone detached itself from the dark sky.

" We rounded Moorea and came in sight of Tahiti.

" A few hours later day dawned. We approached the reefs at slow speed and, making for Venus Point, we glided into the Papeete channel and cast anchor in the roads without mishap.

" At first sight there is nothing romantic about this little island, nothing that can be compared with the magnificent bay of Rio de Janeiro, for instance.

" But I gazed at it in deep emotion — without a thought of comparison. It is the top of a mountain which was submerged at the time of the Deluge; only the extreme summit was left above water. A family sought shelter there (no doubt) and founded a race. And then the coral has built itself up around the new island. It has continued to spread, but preserves its original aspect of loneliness and submission, an aspect which is set off by the vastness of the ocean.

" At ten in the morning I presented myself to the Governor (the Negro Lacascade), who received me as a person of importance. This honour I owed to the mission with which the French Government had entrusted me. I don't know why.

" An *artistic* mission, no doubt; but in the Negro's eyes this word was only a synonym for espionage, and I did all I could to disabuse him of his error, but

in vain. His whole entourage shared his view, and when I told them my mission was unsalaried, nobody would believe me."

Gauguin was disappointed with the capital of Tahiti. Its life was distinguished neither by European enterprise and order nor by the beauty and decorative sense of the natives. Everything was half-and-half — a blend of European boredom and the natural effortless life of the natives. The characteristics of each race had been effaced; a careless indifference had taken possession of life in Papeete. Moreover, when Gauguin landed, the town was full of excitement and misgiving. The last descendant of the ancient royal race was on his death-bed. He it was who had maintained with dignity the rights of the natives; he had been fully recognized and was respected by the colonial administration, and worshipped by his subjects. But King Pomaré V was the last who in virtue of his natural dignity and royal birth could claim respect in both camps. Even if his advice were not asked, the colonial administration showed him the consideration due to the supreme representative of a whole people and thus to the people itself. He exercised an invisible sway which was incomparably greater than the influence the French Government had conceded him, and he had known how to use it for the benefit of the immigrants as well as of the natives. His death betokened a change, and it was not easy to say which direction this would take.

" The King died a few days after my arrival; his funeral has had to wait till everyone in the island and the neighbouring islands could be notified.

" You cannot imagine what a funeral it was. A group from each village sat on the grass singing in turn their famous *hyménées* (choral chants in several parts), and this went on all night. For anyone fond of music this is a real treat, as this people has extraordinary musical gifts. Two chants, man and woman, alternating on a shrill note; other parts forming an accompaniment with extraordinary harmonies. A group of men, basses, imitate the sound of the drum, simply to give the rhythm (a very characteristic rhythm). No, it is impossible to imagine anything more harmonious and abstract. Not one of them sings a false note.

" The hearse, covered with flowers, was drawn by mules which the artillery had decked with nets of black wool. On arriving at the grave in the wood, the priests and chiefs delivered speeches in Tahitian.

" I am writing to you in the evening. This silence of the Tahitian night is stranger than all the rest. It does not exist anywhere else; not a bird's cry to disturb its peace. Here and there a great dry leaf falls to the ground, but without giving you the idea of noise. It is more like the passing of a spirit. The natives often roam about at night, but silently, with bare feet. Always this silence! I understand how these people can sit by the hour, by the day, without

saying a word, gazing at the sky in melancholy. I feel how all this is about to envelop me, and at this moment I have an extraordinary sense of repose. . . .

" What a beautiful night it is! Tonight thousands of individuals are doing the same as I; they let life glide on and their children grow up without their aid. All these people go about everywhere, into any village, along any road, sleep in some house, get a meal and so on, without even saying thank-you, and are ready to return it. And we call them savages! They sing, they never steal, my *door is never shut*, they don't plant themselves on you. A couple of Tahitian expressions characterize them: *Ia ora na* (good-day, good-bye, thanks) and *O na tu* (I don't care, what does it matter? etc.). And we call them savages.

" Don't think me an egoist for leaving you, but let me live like this for a time. Those who reproach me do not know all there is in an artist's nature; why should they pester us with duties like their own? We do not pester them with ours.

" I still think of you all with tenderness."

Gauguin had not been many weeks in Papeete before discovering that it was not the place to give him the inspiration he wanted. The Europeans and the natives had infected one another, making their intercourse an indolent and blunted compromise, which reduced all activity to the barely necessary. The

Maori opposes a happy serenity to all unforeseen events and capricious manifestations on the part of the elements. Without being exactly indifferent they consider the case and say: " *O na tu,*" which is as much as to say: " It doesn't concern me, it's nature's affair to straighten it out." In these islands nature only shows her best sides; there are no beasts of prey, no venomous snakes, no dangerous insects to speak of, that need be feared, no catastrophes to be avoided. The worst trouble is the sudden hurricanes and the floods they occasion; but these are not to be resisted, and next day the sun shines as brightly as before in the cool breeze. All that has to be done is to clean up the mess, put the houses back in their places, and then everything looks after itself — for the Maori.

But to the European *O na tu* is a dangerous poison, a convenient catch-word for " I don't care," " Let it go at that," which undermines their inclination for work and reduces them to veranda loungers, content to let things slide and take to their absinthe when they have set the wheels going for the daily round. The satisfaction of their natural requirements makes no great demand on them; nature is accommodating, and never more so than in the person of the native woman, who is remarkable for her good looks and regards it as a matter of course to abandon herself to a man if he asks her. And if she likes him she comes back, just as naturally as she stays away if he is indifferent to her. But in her relations with the Euro-

pean, who acts according to his prejudices and therefore by calculation, the Maori woman with her excellent natural instinct learns to calculate in her turn and she soon sees that the fact of being *vahiné* to a white man gives her a special position which entitles her to make demands. If she does not discover this at once for herself, the enterprising traders of the islands — the Chinese — are there to make it clear to her. But her natural instinct becomes blunted, and this is still more so with her children by the white men, who cannot be turned loose in their native state like the legitimate Maori children, but become hangers-on of the semi-European community, and to them *O na tu* means: " Let it all slide."

All this Gauguin saw and experienced, and his vigorous nature reacted against it. And King Pomaré's death gave him a hint that the romance of the South Sea Islands was nearing its end. During the actual funeral ceremony he had witnessed the Maori tradition in all its glory, but on the morrow it had sunk into the ground, and the daily life of Papeete had resumed its lazy course.

" And everything fell back into the old groove. We were only a king the less. With him there vanished the last trace of former customs and greatness. With him the Maori tradition died. It was an end indeed. Alas, civilization triumphed, the military spirit, business and officialdom.

" A profound melancholy came over me. Here

A YOUNG WOMAN
1890

VAHINE NO TE TIARE

TAHITI, 1891

had I come this long way to find the very thing I had
fled from. The dream that had brought me to Tahiti
had been cruelly unmasked by actuality; it was the
old Tahiti I loved. But I could not bring myself to
believe it was completely wiped out, that this beautiful race had not preserved some of its old glory
somewhere or other. But how was I, alone, without
information or backing, to find the traces of that distant mysterious past, if they still existed? — to recover the fire that was quenched, revive the flame
among all these ashes?

" However badly things may go against me, it is
not my habit to give up the struggle without having
tried everything, even the impossible. My decision
was soon made. I would leave Papeete, go far away
from the European centre. I had a feeling that if
I adopted the natives' life outright, living among
them in the bush, I might at last through patience
overcome their distrust and get to know what I
wanted.

" An officer of gendarmes kindly offered me his
horse and carriage. So one morning I drove off to
find a cabin for myself.

" My *vahiné* accompanied me; Titi was her
name. She was half-English, spoke only a little
French. She had put on her best dress in honour of
the day, a flower behind her ear in Maori fashion,
and her bast hat, which she had plaited herself, was
decorated with a wreath of orange-coloured shells

over a band of braided flowers. With her black hair floating about her shoulders, proud of driving in a carriage, proud of being smartly dressed, and proud of being the *vahiné* of a white man she believed to be both rich and powerful, she was really handsome and there was nothing ridiculous in her great pride, so well does an air of majesty become the faces of this race. Their long feudal history and their time-honoured memories of great chiefs give them an indelible stamp of pride.

" I know very well that according to strictly European ideas her very self-seeking love would scarcely have weighed more than the venal consent of a street-walker, but I discerned something else in it. Those eyes and those lips could not lie. Love is so much in the blood of all Tahitian women, it overshadows all else to such an extent that, self-seeking or not — it is still love."

The cabin Gauguin had hired was situated at Mateiéa, a strip of level ground between the hills and the sea, about twenty-eight miles from Papeete. Coconut palms and breadfruit-trees surrounded the hut. Above the red earth was a lattice-work fence through which he had a view of the radiant yellow beach, the long line of surf where the waves, capped with glittering foam, drew streaks of shining green, shading from light to dark. And far out the dark ultramarine streak of the Pacific was outlined against white clouds floating in a sky whose brightness

changed colour with the hours of the day, vanished, and was reborn with it. Behind the hut the plain extended, flat and open, and on it were groups of coconut palms with slender stems and huge feathery leaves that swayed and turned in the sea breeze with a varied play of colour. And the cloven mountain rose steeply from the plain, giving the final touch to a landscape nature alone had shaped. There the peaceful open plain joined the inaccessible heights where dwelt *Tupapau*, the spirits. The cleft with its thickets of mango-trees and the river as a road was the only approach to the mysterious guardian of the peace and harmony of the place. And as a detached and living part of this nature, in complete accordance with its rhythm, there was the Maori with his powerful naked limbs, a skin which played with the sun's beams and took its colour from them, and a carefree, harmonious movement which betokened a happy agreement with nature.

Gauguin gazed at this scene with emotion. It stirred his artistic dream and gave it life. It was there, right before his eyes as a reality; but the question was whether he himself was fitted to enter into this reality, whether, after all, he would not be left standing outside, alone and a stranger, as the European who merely sees and is conscious of the peace he so sorely longs for, without finding it for himself.

" That evening I went for a walk on the beach and smoked a cigarette. The sun was sinking rapidly

and was already half hidden by the island of Moorea, which was on my right hand. The strong contrasts of light brought out — black against the flaming sky — the mountains, whose jagged peaks were like the battlements of old castles. I wonder if it is not due to some association that I am haunted by this feudal idea in the presence of this landscape? Look at that mountain summit, it has the shape of a gigantic crest. The waves roar round it like a vast mob which never reaches it. Alone — towering above all this ruined greatness stands The Crest — the protector — the neighbour of heaven.

" From it I let my eyes wander to the great abyss of ocean which swallowed up the swarm of the living, guilty of having meddled with the tree of knowledge, guilty of the great sin of understanding. And The Crest itself becomes a head which by some points of resemblance conjures up for me the Sphinx; that mighty cleft, which might be its mouth, smiles, a majestic smile full of irony or pity, at the waves, wherein the past is asleep. The night came suddenly. Moorea slept. Silence. I learned to know the silence of the Tahitian night.

" The beating of my heart was all that could be heard. From my bed, in the light of the moonbeams which crept in, I could distinguish the reeds which at regular intervals formed the wall of the hut. One might imagine it a musical instrument, the reed-pipe of ancient times, which the Tahitian calls *vivo*. The

instrument is silent all day, but now at night, thanks to the moon, it plays to us in memory the dear old melodies. I fell asleep to its notes. Between me and the sky there was nothing but the high, light roof of pandanus-leaves, in which the lizard lives. In sleep I could imagine the free expanse of space over my head, the vault of heaven, the stars. I was so far away from those prisons, the European houses.

" A Maori hut does not drive one into exile, does not shut one off from life and infinite space. And yet I felt lonely. The inhabitants of the district and I watched each other, and the distance between us did not grow less.

" In two days my supplies would run out. What then? I had imagined that money would procure me the necessaries of life. A fond delusion! If one would live one must have recourse to nature. She is rich and she is generous; she does not say no to him who asks for a share of the treasures she hoards, in the trees, the mountains, and the sea; but then one must climb the highest trees, go up into the mountains and return with heavy loads on one's back, one must catch fish, dive to the bottom of the sea and gather the shellfish that cling to the rocks.

" So for the moment I, the civilized man, was inferior to these savages who lived happily around me, where money that is not derived from nature cannot provide the indispensable good things that nature produces. And as I was thinking over my position,

empty of stomach and sad at heart, I caught sight of a native coming towards me with cries and wild gestures. His expressive signs translated his words and I understood that my neighbour was inviting me to dinner. But I felt embarrassed. I shook my head. A few minutes later a little girl came up with some food neatly wrapped in fresh leaves, laid it on my threshold without a word, and departed. I was hungry and I accepted, as silent as she. Soon afterwards the man passed my hut; he smiled at me and without stopping said in a tone of interrogation the single word: ' *Paieu?* ' I guessed: ' Have you had enough? '

" This was the beginning of mutual accommodation between the savages and me. Savages! The word came instinctively to my lips as I gazed on these dark creatures with cannibals' teeth. And yet I was beginning to appreciate their real charm. That little brown head lying there under the cluster of great giromon-leaves — the child who studied me without my knowing it and ran away when I met his eyes. I was the object of their observation, as they were of mine: I, the stranger, who knew neither their language nor their customs, not even the first and most natural accomplishments of life. To them I was ' the savage,' as they were to me. And perhaps it was I who was wrong."

As usual when he came to a new place it took Gauguin a long time to get to work. He had to become quite at home with the place and its inhabit-

ants, and as this was so entirely new it took him longer than usual. He was not satisfied with realizing the pure and simple beauty of the Maoris; he had to try to penetrate their soul in order to understand that expression of something mysterious which corresponded so wonderfully and beautifully with the constant, unalterable mood of their natural surroundings. There was a purely physical calm and harmony about them, which was only broken by little momentary fits of childish caprice; otherwise the only change in this harmony was the gentle hourly shading of their expression from the freshness of the morning to the evening's melancholy, in agreement with the moods of nature. It was as though nature were mirrored in them, possessed them, and dealt with them as she pleased.

The religious ideas of these people were closely connected with nature, and their divinities were the wind, the sun, and the moon; the last of these, *Hina*, was a goddess of supreme importance, as she ruled the night, and at night the *Tupapau* — the spirits of their ancestors — came out to watch over the children of men, and stood by their side either to protect them or to condemn their evil deeds. It was this mystic, ever present connection between nature and mankind that Gauguin sought to reproduce in his art; but he could not be satisfied with observing it, he had to endeavour to reach its very essence; and here, as a reflective European, he shrank from taking

advantage of the Maoris' compliance before he could feel in himself something of their simple directness of soul.

" I began to work at all kinds of studies and sketches, but the landscape dazzled and confused me with its bold and violent colours. Uncertain as ever, I stood from twelve o'clock to two feeling my way. And then in reality it turned out to be so simple to paint it as I saw it, to put a red or a blue on the canvas without so much calculation.

" Golden bodies in the streams charmed me by their form. Why did I hesitate to pour out all this gold and all this sunny joy over my canvas? Hidebound European training, the typical fear of debilitated races for strong direct expression. In order wholly to identify myself with the character of a Tahitian face, with the charm of a Maori smile, I had long wished to do a portrait of one of my neighbours, a woman of unmixed Tahitian blood.

" I seized the opportunity of asking her one day when she had ventured so far as to enter my hut to look at some photographs of paintings. She examined *Olympia* with particular interest.

" ' What do you think of it? ' I asked, for I had learned a few Tahitian words in the months during which I had spoken no French. She replied: ' She's downright pretty.'

" I smiled at this remark, it touched me. She had a sense of beauty. But what would the professors at

I RARO TE OVIRI
1891

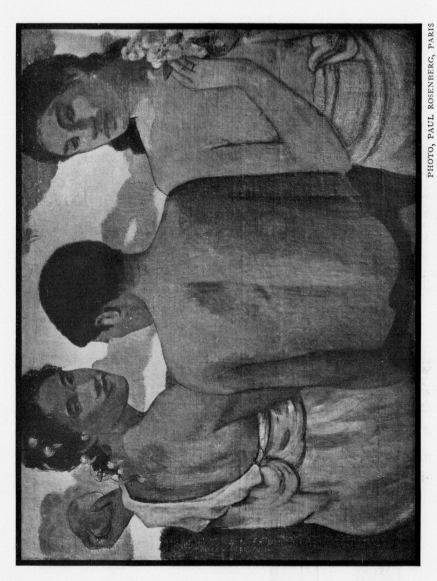

A MAN WITH TWO WOMEN

the École des Beaux-Arts say of her? She suddenly added, breaking the silence that prevails while thoughts are taking shape: ' Is she your wife? '

" ' Yes.'

" I lied. I — Olympia's *tane!*

" While she was absorbed in some religious paintings by the Italian primitives I tried to make a sketch of her, doing my best to fix that enigmatic smile. She made an ugly face and said in an almost resentful tone: ' *Aita* (No),' and disappeared.

" An hour later she was back, handsomely dressed, with a flower behind her ear.

" What had been passing in her mind? Why did she come back? Was it a case of coquetry, the pleasure of yielding, after having resisted? Or the magic attraction of forbidden fruit? Or a caprice pure and simple without any external motive, the sheer whim which is in the blood of the Maori woman?

" I quickly discovered that my study of the model, besides giving me a profound insight into the workings of her mind, placed her physically in my power; it had the effect of a vehement and silent prayer, of an absolute and final conquest.

" She was not exactly pretty according to European ideas, but she was beautiful. All her features showed a Raphaelesque harmony in their curves, and her mouth seemed moulded by a sculptor who could express the joy and passion of thought and kiss. And I saw in her face the dread of the unknown, the

melancholy of bitterness mingled with pleasure, and I saw there the happy possession of a passivity which appeared to be yielding and which in the last resort retained the mastery.

" I worked passionately and in the greatest haste, for I had a feeling that she might change her mind at any moment. I have put into her portrait all that the heart revealed to my eye, and, above all, that which the eye alone would have been incapable of seeing, the glowing wealth of latent forces. . . . Her noble forehead with its prominent lines made me think of Edgar Poe's saying that there is no perfect beauty without a certain singularity in its proportions. And the flower behind her ear was listening to its scent.

" I now worked better and more freely.

" But my loneliness weighed upon me. I saw many young women with calm and carefree eyes, pure, unmixed Tahitians, and I dare say one or other of them was willing to share my existence. But they all wanted to be captured in Maori fashion (*mau* — seize), brutally, without a word. They all, so to speak, desired to be raped. And they actually intimidated me, those at least who were not living with a *tane*. They looked at us men so boldly, with such dignity and pride. And besides, one was told that many of them were ill, suffering from the disease with which the European has infected the savages, as a first and undoubtedly an essential element of his

civilization. And for this reason I did not respond when the old people pointed one of them out to me, saying: ' *Mau tera* (Take her) '; I had not sufficient courage and confidence.

" I sent word to Titi that I should be delighted to see her. And this in spite of her having a terrible reputation in Papeete for having buried one lover after another.

" But the experiment was unsuccessful, and the boredom I suffered in living with this woman, accustomed to the luxuries offered by officials, showed plainly enough what progress I had made in barbarism. After a couple of weeks we parted irrevocably, Titi and I.

" *Alone again!* "

Alone; that meant lonely, and loneliness tormented Gauguin not merely in one way, but in many ways. It called up memories and longings, and with them it roused his conscience; it made him acutely aware how seldom he received news from Europe, and this roused his suspicions. In spite of all their protestations on his departure, his friends seemed to have vanished off the face of the earth. Of course there was something in what Octave Mirbeau wrote of him:

" His thoughts fly to the land of light and mystery which he has already explored. There he believes is to be found a source of art, dormant and untouched, which is new and accords with his dream. That is

why he has such need of solitude, of peace and silence, where he may be better able to listen to himself and will have a greater sense of being alive."

What Mirbeau wrote was true, but Gauguin never intended that he should be forgotten on that account. He had not fled from civilization in order to bury himself, in order that his name might be blotted out. He had not gone into exile. It was by no means his intention to sit on a desert island and make poetry for himself, to build his hut and live at peace without troubling others with what he had at heart. On the contrary: he wished to transform their views, to teach them that life had greater passions, joys, and sorrows than those that found expression in a civilization where Christianity and prejudice barred natural illusions. He wished to bring new fire to the dying flame. Had not Mirbeau said of him again:

" Paul Gauguin is a very peculiar and disconcerting artist who makes no appeal to the public and whom the public therefore does not understand. I have often promised myself to speak about him. I don't know how it is, but one never has time for anything nowadays. And besides, I dare say I have shrunk from such a task, being afraid of falling short in my explanation of a man for whom I have the highest and most respectful esteem. To give a brief and rapid account of an art which is so complicated and so primitive, so clear and so obscure, so barbaric and so refined as Gauguin's, is not that imprac-

ticable — that is to say, beyond my powers? To render such a man and such a work comprehensible would demand an explanation too exhaustive for the space of a newspaper article. I believe, however, that Gauguin's work itself will stand out in a brilliant light if I first touch upon his intellectual experiments and describe briefly his extraordinary and adventurous life. . . .

" Wherever Gauguin may wander he may be assured that our sympathy will accompany him."

But apart from the kind and practical Monfreid's letters, which were often full of good advice, especially as regards his consumption of cigarettes and alcohol, he saw little sign of sympathy from any other quarter.

In his last letter Monfreid had told him that Juliette had given birth to a girl. Poor child, what would happen to her with such a ruffian of a father? And yet — was she not a beautiful manifestation of the course of nature and the persistence of life? Look, for instance, here in Tahiti, how children are greeted with the greatest joy and shown with pride. The idea took possession of him, inspired him. He set to work upon his first large composition in the island. The proud mother in the foreground of a luxuriant landscape with the child perched on her shoulder, and in the background three women paying homage: *Ia orana Maria* — Hail, Mary! But a little aureole about the child's head suggests that he has not yet

entirely resigned himself to barbarism. He is still
haunted by the old refrains; he has not yet adapted
himself wholly to the life around him. He is lonely
and haunted by memories; they pass in and out of
his hut, leaving behind an emptiness which tortures
him as he lies watching the moonbeams as they play
the *vivo* on the lattice wall.

" Within me they are singing, far and near, the
vivo and my heart. And I walked far towards the
ocean, with my memories and my hopes; towards
the wonderful ocean whose deep roar around the
island tells of silence, whose deep roar around the island is like an impenetrable wall brooding over the
place to which I have withdrawn in my exile, and,
full of a feeling of youth, I stretch out my arms to
space. Far away they are singing, both the *vivo* and
my heart."

With a feeling of youthfulness he stretches out his
arms to space; there he can find renewal, and he feels
strong forces within him which will enable him to
reach it, but not in solitude. Not alone. The yawning
emptiness of the hut brings sleepless nights and de-
presses him so that in the daytime he resorts to stimulants which impair his health, especially with his
poor diet, which he can only attend to by fits and
starts. When he goes into Papeete to buy provisions
it invariably ends in a spree among the Europeans,
and he returns ill and exasperated to his hut, which
receives him with the chill of loneliness, with an in-

TWO WOMEN
TAHITI, 1892

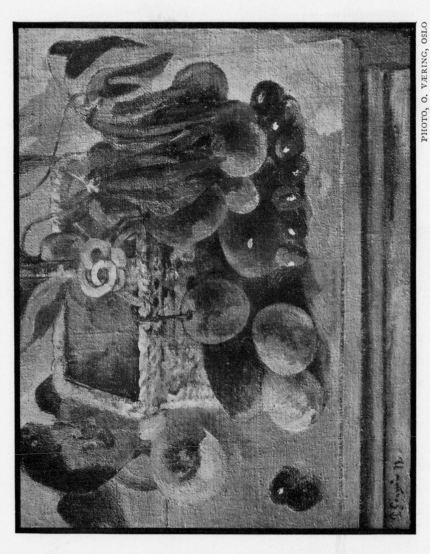

FRUIT
TAHITI 1892

jured look of desolation which does not invite repose.
Conscience lurks in every corner, like a spider watching for his thoughts to be caught in its web. His heart
is racing and demands a sedative. *O na tu* — well,
what does it matter? And after a leaden sleep comes
the nightmare, making one start out of bed and
awaken to a new day. Alone.

But one day the warning came: a violent vomiting
of blood obliged Gauguin to seek medical attention
in Papeete, and fortunately he applied to the only
Frenchman on the island, de Chassagnol, the senior
physician at the hospital, who understood his case
and could appreciate him as a man.

But when he returned to his hut it was as lonely
as before and he was still alone.

" For some time I had been in a gloomy mood and
it coloured my work. To tell the truth, many of my
studies were failures, but cheerfulness was what I
lacked above all.

" Several months had passed since I sent Titi
away; for several months I had not heard the chatter
of my *vahiné*, constantly asking me the same questions about the same things, to which I always replied with the same stories. And this silence had no
very happy effect on me.

" I decided to go away, to set out on a tour round
the island, without making any fixed plan. While I
was making parcels of things I might want on the
tour and putting all my studies in order, my neigh-

bour and landlord, the friendly Anani, stood watching me uneasily. At last he made up his mind to ask if I was preparing to leave. I answered no, I was only getting ready for a few days' trip and I should soon be back. He did not believe me and began to weep. His wife came up and said she loved me. I needed no money to live among them; one day I might find rest for ever *there* — and she pointed to a spot ornamented with a little shrub near the hut.

" And I felt a longing to rest there for ever; at any rate no one would ever come and disturb me there.

" ' You Europeans,' added Anani's wife, ' you always promise to stay, and when at last we've grown fond of you, you go away! You assure us you will come back, but you never do! '

" ' But I can swear that I intend to come back in a few days. Afterwards ' — for I dared not lie — ' afterwards we shall see.'

" At last I got away.

" I left the road which runs along the beach and struck into a narrow path through the bush that extends a good way up into the mountains, arriving at a little valley whose inhabitants lived in the old Maori fashion. They were calm and happy. They dreamed, they loved, they slept, sang, and prayed, and I could clearly see in my mind's eye the statues of their female goddesses, though there were none there. Statues of Hina and festivals in honour of

the moon goddess. The image is forty feet high and ten feet from shoulder to shoulder, made of a single block of stone. On its head is a huge stone shaped like a cap, of reddish colour. Around it they dance according to the ancient rite — *Matamua* — and the *vivo* changes its tone, now bright and gay, now sad and veiled, as the hours go by.

" I went on. At Taravao, the extreme point of the island, a gendarme lent me his horse and now I went rapidly along the east coast, which is little visited by Europeans. In Faone, a little district that you come to just before Itia, I heard a native call to me: ' Hey! you man who makes men ' (he knows I am a painter), ' *haere mai ta maha* (come and eat with us),' the Tahitian formula of politeness.

" I did not require pressing, so attractive and gentle was the smile accompanying the invitation. I got off my horse; my host took it and tied it to a branch, without any servile politeness, deftly and as a matter of course. We both entered a hut where were assembled men, women, and children sitting on the ground as they chatted and smoked.

" ' Where are you going? ' asked a handsome Maori woman of about forty.

" ' I'm going to Itia.'

" ' What do you want there? '

" I don't know what prompted me, and perhaps I told her the real, the secret object of my journey, without knowing it.

" ' To find a wife,' I answered.

" ' There are many good-looking ones at Itia. Will you have one of them? '

" ' Yes.'

" ' If you like I will give you one. She is my daughter.'

" ' Is she young? '

" ' Yes.'

" ' Is she healthy? '

" ' Yes.'

" ' Very well, go and fetch her.'

" The woman went. After a quarter of an hour, which was spent in bringing in the Maoris' wild bananas, prawns, and a fish, she came back accompanied by a tall girl with a little package in her hand. Through her gown, which was of a very transparent pink muslin, one could see the golden skin of her shoulders and arms. Two buds stood out boldly on her breast. I did not recognize in her charming face the type I had hitherto found prevalent in the island; her hair, too, was somewhat unusual, thick as a jungle and slightly crisped. In the sunlight it was an orgy of colour.

" In the course of the conversation I found out that she belonged to Tonga. When she had seated herself at my side I asked her some questions.

" ' You are not afraid of me? '

" ' *Aita* (No).'

" ' Will you live in my hut — for good? '

" ' *Eha* (Yes).'

" ' You have never been *ill?* '

" ' *Aita.*'

" That was all. My heart throbbed as the girl without changing a feature arranged the food that was offered me on a great banana-leaf before me on the ground. I ate with a good appetite, but I was preoccupied and ill at ease. This young girl, this child of about thirteen, captivated me and frightened me. What was passing in her soul? It was I — so old compared with her — who hesitated when the moment arrived for signing a contract so hastily conceived and concluded; perhaps, I thought, her mother has issued her orders, perhaps it is a bargain they have discussed between them. And yet I saw quite plainly in this great child the marks of independence and pride which are characteristic of her race. What did most to ease my mind — and here it was impossible to be mistaken — was that she had the demeanour, the serene expression, which in young people accompanies an honourable and praiseworthy action. But the touch of mockery about her mouth, which, by the way, was kind and sensitive and tender, told me that if there was any danger it threatened me, not her.

" I will not venture to say that my heart was not contracted by a strange feeling of anxiety, by a sickening fear, by a real terror, as I stepped across the threshold of the hut.

" I took my horse and mounted. The girl followed me; her mother, a man, and two young women — her aunts, she said — also attended me.

" We were making for Taravao, five and a half miles from Faone.

" When we had covered the first mile someone said ' *Parahi teie* — Stop here.' I dismounted and we entered a big and well-kept hut, rich in this world's goods: handsome mats laid over hay. A couple lived here, still young and extremely amiable. My fiancée sat down beside the woman and introduced her to me: ' This is my mother.' After that fresh water was silently poured into a cup from which we all drank in turn, as though it were some rite in a family religion. Whereupon she whom my fiancée had introduced as her mother said to me with moist eyes and a look of emotion:

" ' You are kind? '

" I answered — not without some scruples, after searching my conscience:

" ' Yes.'

" ' Will you make my daughter happy? '

" ' Yes.'

" ' Let her come back here in a week. If she is not happy, she will leave you.'

" A long silence. At last we went out and I mounted again and went on, still followed by my escort. On the way we met people who were ac-

quainted with my new relations, and they said to the girl, as they greeted her:

" ' Aha, so you're *vahiné* to a Frenchman! Be happy. Good luck to you! '

" There was doubt in their looks.

" There was one thing that puzzled me: how could it be that Tehura — that was my wife's name — had two mothers? So I asked the one who had first offered her:

" ' Why did you lie to me? '

" Tehura's mother answered:

" ' The other is also her mother, her foster-mother, the one who looks after her.'

" I sat in the saddle plunged in reverie, and the horse, feeling no firm hand on the reins, walked unsteadily, stumbling over the big stones.

" At Taravao I returned the horse to the gendarme. The gendarme's wife, a Frenchwoman, said to me, not with any spiteful intention, but tactlessly: ' So I see you're taking a prostitute with you? '

" And her contemptuous eyes stripped the girl, who replied with proud indifference to this offensive scrutiny. For a moment I watched the symbolical sight presented by these two women: decay and fresh flowering, the law and trust, the artificial and the natural, and upon this she blew the breath of lying and spite. At the same time it was the opposition of two races, and I was ashamed of mine. It

seemed to me that it soiled the beautiful sky with a cloud of dirty smoke, and I turned my eyes away quickly to let them dwell on and be gladdened by the glory of that living gold which I loved already.

" The parting with her family took place at Taravao in the house of the Chinaman who sells everything — human beings as well as animals.

" We — my fiancée and I — took the public coach, which put us down fifteen miles farther on, at my home in Matarea.

" My wife was not very talkative — rather melancholy and inclined to scoff. We scrutinized each other all the time, but I was soon vanquished in this duel and she remained impenetrable to me. It was of little use my determining to keep control over myself so as not to interfere with my clearness of vision; it was not long before my feelings made an end of my earnest resolutions, and in a short time I was an open book to Tehura.

" Thus — at the expense of myself and my own person, so to speak — I gained experience of the deep abyss that separates an Oceanic soul from a Latin, and particularly a French soul. The Maori soul does not surrender itself at once, much patience and study are required before one can gain possession of it. At first it evades and confuses one in a thousand ways, enveloping itself in laughter and caprice; and, while one allows oneself to be captivated by this outward appearance, as though it were the mani-

festation of her true inwardness without a thought of playing a part, she examines one with calm assurance under cover of her laughing nonchalance, her child-like thoughtlessness.

" A week went by during which I was filled with a childishness which was quite foreign to myself. I loved Tehura and told her so, which made her smile; she knew it very well! In return she seemed to love me — but never said so. But now and then at night Tehura's skin shed a golden radiance.

" On the eighth day — to me it seemed as if we had just entered the hut together for the first time — Tehura asked my leave to go and visit her mother at Faone: it was a promise. I acceded sorrowfully, tied up some piastres in her shawl so that she might pay for her journey and buy rum for her father, and accompanied her to the coach.

" To me it was like a farewell. Would she come back? The loneliness of my hut tortured me. I could not concentrate my thought on a single piece of work.

" Some days went by, then she came back."

From this time on, Gauguin passed some happy months in full work. He lived as a Maori, dressed as one, with the *pareo* about his loins, otherwise naked. His artistic dream was now completely realized and every day he penetrated more deeply into its essence. He lived in the present, with a happy consciousness of being free to follow out his artistic idea; and every whim, every temperamental mani-

festation of the child Tehura inspired him while at the same time it appealed to his masculine instinct. All the changing moods of this woman, whose attraction for him was purely sensual, were in accord with nature; she was one with nature, a part of it.

She had all the caprice and mystery of nature; she was light and darkness, day and night. She had the bright laughter of the daytime, and its tears; she had the rapturous silence of the night, and its demonic dread.

" One day I was obliged to go to Papeete. I had promised to be back the same evening, but the carriage I took only brought me half-way, so I had to walk the rest and it was one o'clock at night when I reached home.

" We happened to be short of oil; I was just going to get in a fresh supply.

" When I opened the door the lamp was extinguished, the room was in darkness. I felt a sudden fear and suspicion: the bird had flown. I hurriedly struck a match, and then I saw. — Motionless, naked, lying at full length on her stomach, Tehura stared at me with terror-stricken eyes and seemed not to recognize me. I, too, stood still for a few moments in strange uncertainty. Tehura's terror infected me, it was as though a phosphorescent light radiated from her fixed, staring eyes. I had never seen her so beautiful, never had her beauty appeared so impressive. And in this semi-darkness, which un-

doubtedly was peopled with dangerous apparitions, with obscure imaginations, I was afraid of making any movement that might change the child's terror into paroxysm. Could I tell what she took me for at that moment? With my agitated face might I not be one of the demons or spectres, the *Tupapaus*, with which the legends of her race fill sleepless nights? Did I know what she really was? So violent was the feeling that had seized her, under the physical and mental sway of her superstition, that it converted her into a being utterly strange to me, utterly different from all I had seen before.

" At last she came to herself and I did my utmost to calm her and restore her confidence. She listened to me, sulkily, and said in a voice shaken by sobs:

" ' Don't ever leave me alone again without a light.' "

So absorbed was Gauguin in his attempt to penetrate the primitive soul and thoughts of the Maori that for a time he forgot his own nature; like the natives he lived in the present and in his work and was content. But the past, which he thought he had left behind, overtook him, and at the same time the future and its ambitious aims began to call upon him.

His financial position was becoming difficult, and this brought out the European; he was reminded of his requirements and of his dependence on his homeland, and learned by painful experience that his physique was not equal to the primitive life and that

he could not adopt the Maoris' idea of *O na tu*, though he longed to be able to say like them: " It doesn't concern me, nature will look after it." A longing which was never satisfied and never could be. A tragic and dramatic longing, which intensified his sense of the beauty of his dream and invested it with majesty and greatness. A bitter longing, which set up a struggle within him so that he could never rest from the effort to penetrate the mystery which was himself. And he attacked it courageously, trying always to take the consequences of his actions; he even considered that he always acted logically and after due consideration, never rashly or thoughtlessly. But he was constantly landed in the financial quagmire, like the European he was; and his future prospects alone could rescue him from it.

In spite of his constantly increasing financial difficulties he worked like a madman, and in a way this brought him a rest from his anxieties, since here he was dealing with that side of his adventure which was in his own control and which he could make tangible, with a view to the future. And here he felt on surer ground than ever before; he was now fully convinced that he had reached his goal. He had only to hold out another year and he would be able to convince them at home. All he asked for was a little encouragement and a little support, particularly from his family, who were always included in his future plans.

Although Mette's letters had grown calmer and more accommodating, they were not altogether of a nature to cheer him. She gave him to understand far too often that his view of the situation was different from hers; that it was the view of an artist.

" You are right; I am an artist. There is nothing stupid about you. I am a great artist and I know it. It is because I know it that I have borne so much suffering in order to keep on my course; otherwise I should consider myself a rascal. Which, by the way, I am in the eyes of many people. Well, what does it matter! What vexes me most is not so much my poverty as the hindrances it puts in the way of my art, which I cannot get to come right, as I should be able if my arms were not tied by poverty.

" You tell me I am wrong to live so far away from the artistic centre. No, I am right; I have known for a long time what I am doing and why I am doing it. My artistic centre is in my brain and nowhere else. I am strong because I have never allowed myself to be deflected by others and all I do comes from within myself. Beethoven was deaf and blind, he was completely isolated, and thus his works are the expression of the artist living on a planet of his own. Look what has happened to Pissarro; as a result of always trying to be ahead of and abreast of everything he has lost every scrap of personality and his whole work lacks unity; it just follows the movement of the day, from Courbet and Millet to the little

fellows who work like chemists with an accumulation of little dots. No, I have an aim and I keep it constantly before me. I am the only logical one, and for that reason I shall find very few who will follow me for long.

" Poor Schuffenecker, he reproaches me with being entirely under the sway of my inclinations. But if I did not act thus, how could I bear even for a year this struggle to the death that I have undertaken? My acts, my painting, etc., are always abused at the moment, and in the end I am acknowledged to be right. And then it's the same over again. I believe I am doing my duty, and strengthened by this I refuse to accept any advice, any reproach. The conditions in which I work are unfavourable and one has to be a *colossus* to do what I am doing in these conditions. I wish to dwell on this subject, and if I have spoken of it at such length it is because I know that at the bottom of your heart you are interested in these questions; you have taken a spite against them because they have brought worry and work on you and because people have given you flattering accounts of other callings. If some of them are advantageous, there are plenty which don't bear looking at, in business, etc., and no way out. Whereas art, after all, has its great day. That's not much, I know; but confess that in your heart you are flattered at being the wife of a man who is somebody.

" I have worries enough here and if I were not

sure it was *necessary for my art* I should stay here no longer.

" The want of food is destroying my digestion and I am growing thinner day by day. But I must continue the struggle, without a break. You have no trust in the future, but I have. Because I will have it; otherwise I should have put a match to the powder-barrel long ago. To hope is to live. I must live in order to do my duty to the full, and I can only do it by adding strength to my illusions, bringing hope into my dreams. Day by day as I eat my dry bread, washed down with a glass of water, I can gradually persuade myself that it is a beefsteak.

" Do not take it amiss if I stick to my idea of staying here another year. I am hard at work; I know the soil now, the scent of it; and the Tahitians, whom I draw enigmatically, are none the less Maoris and not Orientals from the Batignolles. It has taken me nearly a year to understand them, and now that I have got there (my foot in the stirrup), I am to give it up. Enough to drive one mad.

" I am pretty well satisfied with my most recent works and feel that I am beginning to get hold of the Oceanic character. I can assure you that what I have done has not been done by anyone else and that it is unknown in France."

Both in his letters to his wife and in those to his friend Monfreid, Gauguin exaggerated the frugality of his diet considerably. It gave him a certain pleas-

ure thus to emphasize the contrast between his former and his present habits, for to tell the truth the
Maoris' diet appealed more to his eye than to his
palate; and at the same time it gave him an opportunity of pointing out how ridiculous his position
was, compared with what it ought to be. He was not
calling for their pity, but for their reflection. He
wanted to make them understand that modesty was
not to be expected of him and that his choice of a
primitive life did not mean that he had reduced his
claims. He had adopted this life for the sake of his art
and because he despised the Europeans' fear of primitive instincts. But if they thought the primitive had
anything to do with the frugal, they were entirely
mistaken. On the contrary, in the primitive were
latent the great forces which produce the surplus,
the forces which make greater demands on experience than can be satisfied by ordinary humdrum life.
He was an artist; that is, a person who had no need
to obey other laws than those dictated by his natural
instincts, laws which he could justify by his own
personality.

Gauguin knew very well that he made great demands on the understanding of others; but on the
other hand they would have to acknowledge one day
that he made great demands on himself, and that he
had paid dearly for satisfying them. They must not
therefore be allowed to harbour the idea that Tahiti
as he represented it was a paradise for himself; and

those people in particular who pottered about in
their commonplace comfort, whose life was filled
with prosaic needs, must be taught to see how painful it was to have to isolate oneself entirely from their
world, which had also been his, in order to witness
the fulfilment of his dream, like a fairy-tale unfold-
ing itself before his very eyes. A fairy-tale of which
he was himself only a spectator, or at the best a robber
who plundered its fertility.

When Michelangelo strove to create physical
beauty in his works it was perhaps due in great measure to his being himself ugly and deformed. If he,
Gauguin, constantly aimed at the simple and primitive, it was possibly owing to his being himself
so complicated and many-sided. His longing gave
primitive beauty a dramatic and majestic bearing,
and his art was a continual struggle to penetrate the
soul of this beauty and the mystery it preserved even
in surrender.

" I am doing a nude of a young girl. In this pose
it would only require a touch to make her indecent.
And yet I want her like this, the lines and the movement interest me. So I am putting a dash of terror
into the head. There must be a pretext for this terror,
or it must be explained, and that in accordance with
the Maoris' character. This people has traditionally
a very great fear of the spirits of the dead. Any of our
girls would be afraid of being surprised in this position. (Nothing of the sort among the women here.)

I have to explain this terror with the minimum of literary aids, such as used to be employed. So this is what I do. A general effect of harmony, dark, mournful, and alarming, suggesting the toll of a funeral bell. Violet, dark blue, and orange yellow. I paint the linen a greenish yellow, first because this savage's linen is different from ours; secondly because it suggests artificial light (a Kanaka woman never goes to bed in the dark), but I won't have a lamplight effect (it's too common); thirdly, this yellow joining together the orange yellow and the blue completes the musical chord. In the background are some flowers, but they ought not to have a look of reality, being imaginary. I am making them look like sparks of fire. To the mind of the Kanaka the phosphorescent lights at night are the spirits of the dead; they believe in them and are afraid of them. And to finish the picture I put in the ghost, very simply, just an ordinary little woman; because the girl, knowing nothing of the ghosts of the French stage, is only able to connect the spirit of the dead with the dead person herself; that is to say, some person known to her.

" So here you have a little text which you can learn, to answer the critics when they bombard you with their spiteful questions."

As far as his art was concerned, Gauguin found inspiration enough in the chances of adventure, but his ambition had other aims and grew with every success

MANAO TUPAPAU
1892

VAHINE NO TE VI
1892

he achieved in his work. Nor could he rest satisfied even in this; he had plans in his head of removing to the Marquesas Islands. From the yarns of a blustering sea captain he had heard that as regards beauty and disposition the women of Tahiti were only a dying flame compared with those of the Marquesas. He was fascinated by the idea of visiting those islands, but ambition gained the day and he decided to finish off his work in Tahiti and then sail for home. He would show everybody who thought he was safely disposed of in the ends of the earth that he had no intention of turning hermit or of forgetting that he had slipped out of their memory. He had assured them that he was a great artist, and Charles Morice, Émile Bernard, Armand Séguin — in short, all the mediocrities — seemed to believe it. He would show them that he was still alive and was so great an artist that he had no need of their encouragement or of their way of appropriating his art for the benefit of a common idea; and above all it should be brought home to Mette at last that he was a great artist.

" I am longing to see you all again and to take a little rest. But we must be reasonable. A voyage like this is no light matter, no pleasure trip. I must get all I can out of it, and it is to be the end of all my roving. Be patient a little while longer; it will be for the good of you all."

He had some qualms of conscience with regard to his only faithful friend, Daniel, whom he still had

to burden with all his difficulties. But what was
he to do? — none of the others answered him, not
even those who actually owed him money.

Whenever, at intervals of many weeks, he saw the
smoke of the mail-boat rising behind Moorea, his
heart palpitated with excitement and impatience.
Would all the chances he had been waiting for turn
up? If not, it meant more letters, more urgent in-
sistence, and then another long wait for a reply. Only
very rarely were the replies satisfactory and hardly
ever did they contain good news. But at the end of
1892 he had a letter from Mette informing him that
the Committee of the Free Exhibition in Copenhagen, which had just been formed as a protest
against the official exhibition, wished him to be
represented when they opened in the following
February, together with works by van Gogh. Here
was a chance; at any rate it was an encouragement
which he would never have looked for from that
quarter. Now more than ever it was a case of making
a great effort to get back. But it could not be done
without money, so Daniel must be pressed into the
service; and prayers were no longer of any use, it
had come to threats, the threat that he would soon
be back. He could have wished that his friend was
less cautious and unbiased, more pushing, that he
would lay more stress on Gauguin's indignation at
the wrongs he had to suffer. Apparently Daniel was

not even convinced of his being obviously in the right. So it was no use his treating the matter good-naturedly, if he wanted to hurry things on. The people at home must be given the idea that he was sitting on a volcano, while the beautiful fairyland was spread out at his feet. And in fact that was how he really felt, so it was not difficult to find words for it in his letters.

" *My dear Daniel,*

" I have just received 700 francs and they will give me some butter for my spinach. If I had had them a month or two ago I should have been off to the Marquesas to finish my work, and the most interesting part of it. But I am tired, and the boat for the Marquesas does not leave for a month and a half. Besides, I am expecting by next mail what will cover my voyage home, etc. All these things keep me hanging about and prevent my making a decision. I have wiped out the Marquesas and shall turn up one of these days in Paris. I wrote to Sérusier several months ago, sending him a reply to be forwarded to N—. I have heard nothing. Has Sérusier received my letter?

" My God, how difficult it is to do business by correspondence! For two years I haven't been able to clear up this affair of N—. I promise you that in a fortnight after my arrival I shall have got to the bottom of it.

" What a queer fellow that Z— is! He could not take the opportunity of writing me a line himself when he was sending me money.

" What an age this is of human stupidity and vanity! This little being is furious at seeing me get ahead of him in painting and thinks it's my fault that he's behindhand. Yet he has no cause to complain of his luck. Born to be a humble workman or concierge, or a small shopkeeper, he has managed without an effort (it has all come from outside) to make himself a gentleman and an owner of house property.

" As a painter he had a temperament below zero. After having been an admirer of Baudry and his like he has gone about from contrariness or business instinct (the Salon would not accept him). Well then, as you know, he preached the holy war, meaning to follow me and go beyond me; but I'm not so easy to follow with my seven-league boots, and he has stopped on the way, puffing and blowing. If he would even obey; but he insists on working after his own head and tries to be original in spite of all. Hence all the dissensions that you know about. He reproaches me with being self-willed and he fears for his liberty, etc. A contradiction: he wants to walk on his own feet and reproaches me for not having pushed him along. All this is sad, and above all petty.

" You are having troubles of your own, you are

going through the period of failure. Sometimes that's an excellent thing. At this distance I can't form any opinion or offer any advice. I will have a look at it on my return. Don't take it too much to heart and keep on working.

" Thanks for the colours. I have some left and shall not want any more. For the last two months I have done no actual work; I content myself with observing, reflecting, and making notes. My output in a stay of two years, some months of which were lost, will be 66 canvases, more or less good — and some ultra-savage pieces of sculpture. That's enough for one man —

" I believe that at the moment I have a better chance of success in Denmark than in France; unfortunately it is a very small country and the resources are very limited. That vein will soon be worked out —

" Moreover today I seem to have quite a following of young men, and they are getting on, I am told; as they are younger and hold more trumps, and are cleverer than I, perhaps I shall be distanced. For catching up with them I count on this new Tahitian stage; that will be a change after my Breton studies and it will take them some time yet to follow me along this road.

" We shall see! Unless I give up painting, which is very likely, as I told you in my last letter.

" You know that infirmity of mine, doing with-

out sleep; many of my children have been the same; impossible to get them to sleep at night.

" My wife writes that Émile, my eldest son, measures 6 feet 5 at the age of eighteen and a half; that's promising. So they'll be able to call him the Great Gauguin."

As soon as Gauguin had made up his mind to return home the moment he had an opportunity of doing so, he lived in two worlds; and although he was honest with himself, he had a distinct feeling that he was not quite honest with the others and that he was playing a double part. This stirred his conscience and led to an inner conflict, but at the same time it touched strings of pity within him. He watched attentively each change of expression in the young woman at his side. Tehura had grown more silent, more thoughtful, her natural dignity had acquired a touch of pride. She showed an interest in the photographs of his children, which were nailed up on a plank in the wall, and she was especially attracted by his eldest son, a fine big boy with bold, frank features. Emil! She too was going to have a son by her *tane;* and he too would be big and strong. He must be called Emil. She asked him. A strange feeling came over Gauguin; he granted her request; but he was to be called Émile with an *e*, like the child in Jean Jacques Rousseau. This eldest son of his new existence, of his fairyland, could be

safely left behind. Nature would take care of him.

" I had to go back to France. Urgent family duties called for my return.

" Farewell, hospitable country, lovely country, the home of freedom and beauty! I leave you two years older, but twenty years younger, more of a *barbarian* than when I came and yet richer in knowledge. Yes, the savages have taught me much, me, the son of an old civilization; much have these ignorant ones taught me of the art of living and the art of being happy.

" As I left the quay, at the moment of sailing, I saw Tehura for the last time. She was sitting on the stone quay with her legs hanging over the side, caressing the salt water with her broad and powerful feet. Tired, still distressed, but calm. The flower she had worn behind her ear had fallen into her lap — withered.

" Here and there were others like her, watching wearily and vacantly the thick smoke of the vessel that carried us away, all of us — their lovers of a day. And through our glasses we thought we could still read upon their lips this old Maori strophe:

" 'Hasten, light breezes from the south and east
That fondly play above my head;
Hasten together to the other isle.
There you will find him who deserted me,
Taking his ease beneath his favourite tree.
Tell him that you have seen my tears.' "

CHAPTER 6

THE voyage from Tahiti was long and wearisome. First a terribly cold spell at Sydney. After that a delay of nearly a month at Nouméa — expensive and mortally tedious for Gauguin, whose only thought was of getting back to France and who had to practise the most severe economy. The boat he was to transfer to carried troops whose time had expired, so he had to change from third class to second — fresh expense. And on entering the Red Sea it was so hot that sleep and waking were merged in one nightmare of apathetic fancies, in which one pursues but never reaches one's aim, and time flies without one's being able to budge from the spot; one goes backwards like a shadow through one's whole existence.

A breeze that brushed the skin like a physical contact started Gauguin out of this unresting somnambulism. Awake and impatient he walked the deck, waiting. In a few days the voyage would be over,

he would be able to leave the narrow deck-plank that he had paced, backwards and forwards, times without number, and thenceforth his road would lead in one direction only.

" *My dear Mette,*

" Here I am at last, arrived at Marseilles safe and well, and I am telegraphing to Daniel to send me if possible enough to pay my railway and hotel expenses. What money I had has all gone on the voyage. As soon as you get this letter write me at length *how everything is going at home* (it will be five months since I had news of you); tell me at the same time what state our finances are in, so that I can make my calculations. Of course all this work that I have brought back cannot be turned into money in a few days and I have some absolutely necessary expenses on arrival. I have had no news of the canvases I sent you (beyond that they duly arrived). But what sort of an impression did they make at the Exhibition in Denmark?

" You must give me a full account of everything so that I may arrange my business in Paris.

" The voyage home was terribly exhausting: the Red Sea in particular was excessively hot and we were obliged to throw three dead passengers overboard, stifled by the heat.

" I am glad to say I am pretty well: for the last six months I have gained a good deal in strength and

put on weight. You will be able to embrace a husband who is more than skin and bones and not too worn out.

" I am writing this on board to save time and shall post my letter as soon as I land.

" I am full of misgivings about my arrival. Is Daniel in Paris just now and can he send me the money? (I have just enough in my pocket to send the telegram and take a cab to bring my baggage to a hotel where I shall wait for the cash.

" I have some weight of baggage, pictures and sculpture, which is going to cost a lot of money!

" Good-bye for the present — write at once —

" I embrace you with all my heart.

" *Paul* "

When Gauguin, after an absence of nearly two years and a half, stood once more on his native soil he felt content. All the bitterness he had accumulated was nothing compared with the expectations he had of the work he had executed in those years. He had been able to work in peace, more or less, and in such conditions as had made his art quite clear to him. Even if he had only four francs in his pocket, he now felt more secure, with firm ground under his feet. All he had to do now was to raise the necessary money for getting to Paris. Two telegrams were sent off — quite unnecessarily. The attentive Daniel had

seen to it that there was money waiting for him at the post office.

On, then, to Paris as quickly as possible. But Paris was empty. Everyone was away, so Gauguin had to arm himself with patience, a thing which was not easy for him. One day he looked in on Durand-Ruel, who received him with great amiability and promised to come up and look at his pictures and possibly to arrange an exhibition.

He had to find a studio and get his pictures ready for showing. At No. 8 rue de la Grande Chaumière there was a good studio to let, and at the dairy just opposite he was able to borrow enough to pay the deposit. The owner of this dairy, Madame Caron, was no ordinary woman and knew Gauguin of old. Besides her milk business she managed a little eating-house, which was frequented by the pupils of the Académie Colarossi, and used to buy, according to her means, some pictures of the artists who interested her; nor was she afraid of helping them in an emergency.

But as Gauguin was in the midst of his preparations for receiving his picture dealer he received information that his uncle Isidore of Orléans had died and that in all probability a little legacy would come his way.

Though it was not very much — thirteen thousand francs — it could not have come at a more con-

venient moment. When one has business with a picture dealer it is important not to be forced to sell one's skin too cheaply. This paltry sum was nothing compared with the capital vested in the pictures he had in store, but it came in very handy to start with and secure the future, and for that it was to be employed. The first and most important thing was to set himself up in a studio where he could receive his friends and people of influence. Unfortunately he could not get all the money paid out at once — always these confounded formalities which prevented one from carrying out one's plans properly. But at any rate he found at No. 6 rue Vercingétorix a fairly large studio which was rather out of the common. It was approached through a big gateway in a high wall facing the street; this led to a large courtyard with a big tree, and then you came to a low building with two studios on the ground floor and three on the first. Access to the first floor was by an outside staircase with a balcony. From the balcony you entered first a little anteroom with an alcove for a bed on one side; from this a glass door led to the studio, which Gauguin lost no time in decorating with a picture in Maori style: *Te Faruru — Maison du Jouir.* The anterior part of the studio was kept in semi-darkness, as a sharp contrast to the strong light from a side window high up in the other half. Gauguin painted the windows chrome yellow. The furniture consisted

of a divan with oriental rugs and a quantity of weapons from the South Sea Islands, all procured in Paris, and the walls were covered with his paintings. A piano and a big photographic camera were the only things to remind one of Paris or Europe. For domestic animals, a monkey and a parrot. And for attendant and mistress, a handsome Javanese named Annah, a well-known model from the studios of Montparnasse.

Certainly this setting was not altogether genuine, but at any rate it supplied a sort of framework to his art, giving it a suggestion of reality without which it might have been interpreted symbolically.

Here Gauguin received visitors at all hours, one may say. His door stood open and he wished it so; he was no grudging host. And in the course of the autumn he had many visitors, some who came out of curiosity, but many more who were interested both in Gauguin's personality and in his art. Even if they did not understand it fully, it gave them a feeling that here new ideas and new forces were being brought to maturity. Everywhere in Europe the nineties were a period of conflict and of reaction against the realism and rationalism of the preceding decades. The movement of the eighties had at last secured the upper hand over formal classicism and a long-deceased romanticism, the stench of whose corpse could no longer be disguised by the incense of

potpourri jars. But so dazzling was the reaction of the eighties in its development, so strict were its artistic exigencies, and so marked was its lucidity that the younger generation turned against it, finding that it did not give them scope for the free play of their sentiments and emotions. While the eighties were marked by a cleaning up and the definite conclusion of a whole century of somewhat confused artistic development, the nineties were distinguished by an experimenting and a new orientation towards something new, based on legends and myths from distant ages and from foreign lands.

Although this was quite alien to Gauguin's own way of thinking — since he only acknowledged the fantasy that was within himself — he had no objection to trying to explain it to others, being convinced that, when once they had understood it, the clear and simple aims of his own art would also be intelligible to them.

They were mostly poets who came to see him; the majority of the painters who had formerly championed his cause now deserted him, seeing him to be useless as an ally or a leader. In fact, some of them, like Émile Bernard and Schuffenecker, actually attacked him; the former from morbid vanity in order to assert his own personality, the latter from frantic despair at having none to assert.

Among painters of note Degas was the only one to perceive Gauguin's great talent. But he never left

his own den or approached others except as an observer.

Gauguin had thus made every preparation for striking the great and final blow for his art when his exhibition opened at Durand-Ruel's in November. A handsomely got-up catalogue with a preface by Charles Morice told of forty-four pictures and two pieces of wood-carving, most of them from Tahiti, with titles in the native language. Everything had been done to arouse interest. But the interest was not there. The attitude of the best critics, though appreciative, was one of suspended judgment, while the public seemed completely bewildered. That section of it which had at last arrived at a comprehension of such modern artists as Manet and Renoir, Monet and to some extent Pissarro, found in Gauguin's pictures a foreign and exotic element which was directly contrary to the homelike and pronouncedly French note that prevailed in the art they had newly discovered. Even Durand-Ruel, who had undertaken the exhibition on the strength of Degas's opinion, having implicit confidence in his artistic judgment, felt somewhat shaken. In any case he found that Gauguin had overrated his works and was asking absurd prices for them. And this annoyed Gauguin. He was not going to be classed with the common herd, he meant to sit among the great.

His mother's fatal " All or nothing " reappeared in the son, and his relations with Durand-Ruel grew

worse and worse, till the picture dealer swore an oath that Gauguin's works should never again be seen upon his walls.

Could these people understand nothing? Was his art too simple for these too refined and witty Parisians?

" Since my Tahitian art has been regarded as incomprehensible, I will try to explain it. My intention was to give the idea of a superabundantly rich and wild nature, a tropical sunshine which sets fire to all around; with this in view I had to provide my figures with a harmonious setting.

" This is a life in the open air, but at the same time an intimate life. In the thickets, in the shady streams, the women whisper in a vast palace decorated by Nature herself with all the wealth of Tahiti.

" Hence these fabulous colours, this flaming but filtered and silent atmosphere.

" But all this doesn't exist!

" Yes, it does; as the equivalent of the greatness, the depth, and the mystery of Tahiti, when you have to express it on a canvas a yard square.

" The Tahitian Eve is very subtle and very shrewd in her naïveté.

" I cannot expound the elusive riddle that hides in the depths of her child's eyes.

" It is not little Pierre Loti's pretty Rarahou, listening to a romance of Pierre Loti played on the guitar and pretty like herself. It is Eve after the Fall,

still able to go naked and unashamed and retaining all her animal beauty of the first day. Motherhood will have no power to disfigure it, for the loins are as strong as before.

" The feet of a quadruped, I dare say.

" As in Eve, the body is still animal. But the head has developed, thought has induced subtlety, love has imprinted that ironical smile on her lips and quite naïvely she searches her memory for the ' Why? ' of today. She turns on you a baffling look.

" This is intangible, I am told. Very well; I accept that."

It was a great encouragement that Degas quite unreservedly showed his admiration for his younger colleague. And he not only admired his art but valued the strength of character Gauguin had shown in pursuing his aim without turning aside or trying to ingratiate himself in any quarter.

" Degas despises theories about art and is never preoccupied with technique.

" At my last exhibition at Durand-Ruel's, *Œuvres de Tahiti*, '91, '92, there were two well-meaning young men who could make nothing of my painting. As respectful friends of Degas they asked him for enlightenment.

" With his kindly smile, so paternal and yet so young, he repeated to them the fable of the dog and the wolf.

" Gauguin, you see, is the wolf."

And within a certain circle of young writers his art attracted a good deal of attention, so that the studio of the rue Vercingétorix soon became much frequented and Gauguin's evening gatherings were much discussed among those interested in art, not infrequently in rather too fantastic terms.

One of the most habitual guests was Charles Morice, whose forgetfulness during Gauguin's absence abroad was quickly forgiven. On meeting a man face to face Gauguin's distrust very soon gave way to his need of confidence and a friendly feeling. The few direct clashes that had occurred in his life had taught him to know and to fear more than anything else his violent and ungovernable temper.

" I prefer to have too much confidence, and to be deceived as a result, rather than to be always distrustful. In the first case I suffer at the moment of deception; in the second I suffer continually."

As literary editor of *Le Mercure de France,* an organ of modern ideas, and as a sort of leader of the Symbolist movement Morice regarded Gauguin as a discovery of his own who was to be brought to the front, rather than as one for whom he had friendly feelings. Morice was a typical representative of the mentality of the nineties: uncertain and tentative, swayed by feeling and sentiment in his artistic form and extremely vulnerable to any sober demand for a logical content to the emotional mysticism in which he loved to enshroud himself. Gauguin always tried

to give a clear impress of reality to his accounts of
the South Sea Islands and the life of the Maoris.
When he talked about them he did so in a simple
and lucid way, in short and terse sentences, which
Morice appropriated and worked up into fantastic
and picturesque descriptions in florid and high-flown
language. So enraptured was he with his own inspiration that he proposed to Gauguin that they should
collaborate on a book on Tahiti: *Noa-Noa* — " O
fragrant land." It was to point the way to the art of
the future, to a new and elusive goal which was the
spiritual aspiration of all.

" A painter's memory, confirmed by plastic evidence and the simplest of narratives. A poet's fancy
— a poet who dreams among the painter's works
while listening to his tale, dreams of the landscapes
and faces that inspired the painter and from these
dreams as, little by little, they take shape, creates
another work of art.

" The memory and the fancy of a painter and a
poet have created this; two wills have given it unity
and harmony, both possessed by the same subject and
by the same profound belief that from the beginning
art has been one and indivisible, and that the future
of any branch of art must lie in a return — through
the magic convolutions of what arabesques? — to
the triumphant cohesion which will again produce the miracle of the glory of all gardens assembled
in one bouquet. — An ineffable aim and yet a sure

one, of which this book gives but a hint; and yet perhaps its prayer may reveal this aim to the soul of the believer, by pointing with two clasped hands the way to paradise."

Obscure but flattering words which for Gauguin threw a ray of light into the darkness which hindered the comprehension of his art, but which at the same time gave some indication of the way by which there was a possibility of getting on terms with people. The important thing was that he should write as much of the book as possible himself, and he threw himself into the task with zeal.

The exhibition at Durand-Ruel's had certainly not answered all expectations, but on the other hand it had not passed unnoticed, and on the whole the critics had been rather favourable than otherwise. And the visits Gauguin had received gave him many proofs that in certain quarters his art had even aroused very great interest.

All he had to do now was to keep this interest warm and to exercise a little patience.

" *My dear Mette*,

" For some time past I have been suffering from rheumatism, from the right shoulder right down to the hand, and I confess I am rather disheartened at the state of things.

" As a matter of fact my exhibition did not turn out as one had a right to expect, but we must look

things in the face. I had fixed very high prices — 2 to 3,000 francs on an average. At Durand-Ruel's I could scarcely do otherwise, considering Pissarro, Manet, etc. But there were many bids as high as 1,500 francs. What is one to say? The only thing to do is to wait, and broadly speaking I was right, for a price of 1,000 francs doesn't seem overwhelming in the present state of the market.

" Don't let us think about it. The important thing is that my exhibition was a very great artistic success; indeed, it aroused fury and jealousy. The press has treated me as it never treated anyone before; that is to say, with elaborate caution and commendation. At the moment, in the eyes of many people, I am the greatest modern painter.

" Thanks for your proposal that I should come to Denmark, but I am tied here for the whole winter by a great deal of work. Many people to receive — visitors who want to look at my pictures — buyers, I hope. A book about my travels, which gives me a lot of work.

" What kills me is this damned struggle for money. The notary is never tired of dunning me, and I am always going to pay back tomorrow the trifling sum I borrowed and promised to repay at the end of October. This paralyses my arm and I can't buy many necessary things. Enough of that!

" Listen to what I propose, and I believe it is the most sensible of all suggestions. Would it not be pos-

sible to rent a fisherman's cottage on the Norwegian coast, where I could work and where you could join me with the children in the holidays? "

He knew that Mette was in constant communication with Schuffenecker, so there was every probability that she was not entirely ignorant of the life he was leading in Paris. But he relied on her sound common sense and her cool and practical nature. To be honest with himself he had to acknowledge that she was his superior in the constancy of her emotions. There had never been a hint in her letters that she distrusted him as a husband, and it could not be denied that suspicion sometimes lurked between the lines of his letters to her. As, for instance, during his stay in Tahiti, when she visited Paris in their common interest and at his own suggestion stayed at Morice's.

" You speak of Morice with an enthusiasm that is very suggestive of a woman in love, and besides that your letter is far more affectionate than usual, as though you had something to be condoned. I hope you have only sinned in thought. I can be jealous, but I have no right to speak, having been separated from you for so long. I can understand that a woman who spends her best years away from her husband may have moments of desire, both carnal and sentimental."

He knew very well that the life he was now

leading gave offence in many quarters and that the rumours in circulation about him were often exaggerated and fantastic, and he himself felt the need of settling down. But the question was in the first place how he was to adopt a more regular existence, shared with his wife and children, so long as his art was looked upon as a curiosity that had no root either in the French spirit or in the artistic forms of the last twenty years. To occupy an isolated position in respectable society with his exigencies and with an uncertain and fitful income was not a tempting prospect. Where money was concerned he had never had a thought of the morrow, even as a banker, but had trusted in his own capacity as an incurable optimist. And he was still the same, where there was visible proof of anything tangible. All he had to do was to wait a little while, but not in isolation; better to be a curiosity surrounded by a little band who were themselves trying new paths and with whom he could be generous as far as his means allowed. But there was also another question: whether in a calm and respectable existence he would be able to follow out the line of his art; whether it would enable him to live as genuinely in accordance with his nature as he was doing now, and to obtain inspiration for new works through direct experience.

For he felt that Tahiti was only a stage in his artistic development, as Brittany had been. He hoped and believed that he could enter upon a new stage.

But how? As things were at present, in an existence which was neither one thing nor the other, he met with no satisfying experiences, everything was based on memory, and that did not give form to his imagination, except when he took to black and white, illustrating and translating the literary and emotional elements that had crept into his painting. Here alone memory could assist him to give free rein to his fancy without being surrounded by the relevant atmosphere.

Perhaps, too, this road would bring him nearer to the public, which either thought him mad or believed he despised it and cared nothing whether it understood him or not; which was an entirely wrong view. The great public was only a neglected child that he longed to take to his heart and overwhelm with his bounty. And until he could do this, art would never bring him complete satisfaction.

" Oh, if the good public would learn to understand a little bit, how I would love it!

" When I see them examine one of my pictures and turn it upside down, I am always terrified they may spoil it, as when they feel their way with a girl, and that my work ever after will bear the trace of this violation.

" And then someone down in the crowd calls out to me: ' Why do you paint? For whom do you paint? For yourself alone? '

" That hits me. I crawl away ashamed."

But the public was now divided into two camps, sharply opposed to each other. One of these supported the official art of the Salon, which was represented to some extent by stiff and dry monumental painting, based on history and literature even in its scenery; and the landscapes were dusty with *genre* and old romantic sentiment; an acquired literary education clung to official art. Against this the Impressionists had reacted, and now that they had conquered a public for themselves, it had become something of a catchword that painting must bear no literary stamp, it must be painting pure and simple. The monumental and decorative element in it must only result from the natural impression and the artistic composition of the picture. It was easy after all to agree upon a formula like this and to understand it. It was really a case of cleverly exploiting the means of artistic expression.

But Gauguin's art fell just midway between these two points of view. He himself reacted against both.

" I am not a scholar, but I am a writer."

His thoughts were in a constant state of activity, but not in any definite direction; experience was wanting to give them a fixed point of departure. If anyone had asked him: " What are you thinking of? " he might have answered: " I don't know." And this made him react against the current demand for dogma. Impressionism was succeeded by Post-Impressionism, Pointillism, Symbolism, and

Raphaelism, and none of these gave room for the free flow of ideas and for the individual's natural craving for experience. A personal idiom simply introduced confusion into the artistic elegance of *l'Art nouveau.*

Gauguin's determined attitude and his unshakable conviction, which he purposely emphasized by ostentatiously dressing and living in defiance of conventional custom, did more to scare people away than to attract them. Most of them, Pissarro in particular, saw in this a mere pose on the part of the former bank clerk. And Pissarro was now a powerful and influential man, in many ways the leader of the *Art nouveau* movement. It was no pose. Only a very few understood that it implied a marked disclosure of Gauguin's soul and individuality, of what lay at the foundation of his art. This art was to be understood directly and not as a part of any artistic movement. Even the majority of those who made an effort to understand him interpreted his art on the basis of ideas which were strangely foreign to him. They dressed him up in borrowed plumes, or at any rate provided him with a tiny fig-leaf, fearing to see how naked he was in reality.

It frequently happened that he felt lonely among his guests in the rue Vercingétorix. Nor did he get much work done; so when the fine weather set in he decided to go to Brittany and try to resume his work there, aided by his more recent experiences.

TWO CHILDREN

BRITTANY, 1894

POÈMES BARBARES
1896

The place he chose was Pont-Aven, where the landlady of the inn, Madame Gloanec, was his good and faithful friend, who would not take it amiss if he arrived accompanied by Annah and the monkey. But his work got on slowly. Although he knew every inch of the place, he now looked at it with other eyes. The firm and shapely curves of the Maoris, the strong elasticity of their movements, were entirely lacking in these powerful, angular Bretons, whose movements were stiff and did not correspond so well with the rhythm of the landscape. Their calm, cold eyes did not afford the wonderful changes of expression of the soft, warm eyes he had been used to.

It was mostly landscapes that he painted; the bold undulation of their lines interested him, but he missed the wealth of colour of the Tahitian landscape. The shivering monkey and the blue lips of the Javanese girl only served to remind him of the lack of sunshine, which did not help him to throw off the bronchitis he was always subject to in Paris. And yet he had no longing to be back in Tahiti. He felt that his future lay here in France; if only his native land would be quick and show him some hospitality. He needed it for the development of his art; friendliness and understanding, and perhaps a home of his own, were the subjects of his day-dreams.

But one day when he had taken Annah with him on a visit to the neighbouring town of Concarneau he fell in with half a score of drunken sailors, who

showed an indelicate interest in the young woman. Not much had been said before Gauguin came to blows with the whole party, and they soon found out that single-handed he was a dangerous opponent in open fight. So one of them hastened a decision by giving Gauguin a kick which broke his shin so that the bone protruded. Some acquaintances came up and saw the sailors in flight and Gauguin lying in the roadway.

Carried into a house, he asked for a cigarette and lighted it; then without a sign of pain he allowed the doctor to set his leg, smoking one cigarette after another. He passed the whole night like this, alone, without calling for anyone, merely struggling with evil thoughts. In the morning he was told that Annah had decamped with his money and keys. He treated it with indifference, nor did he report the sailors' assault. He let it all rip; at any rate while he lay here he could be nothing but a nuisance to his fellow creatures. His only thought was of getting on his feet and away; but the leg was difficult to mend and the wound would not heal.

" *My dear Daniel,*

" No, I don't write very often and everybody complains of it. You see, I have quite lost heart through all my suffering, especially at night, when I don't get any sleep at all. And this being so, of course I've got nothing done; four months wasted and lots of

expenses. However, I have made a firm resolution: to settle in Oceania for good.

" I shall return to Paris in December for the sole purpose of selling the whole caboodle for what it will fetch. (All of it.) If I can manage that, I shall leave not later than February. Then I can end my days in peace and freedom without taking thought for the morrow and without this everlasting struggle with the Imbeciles. This time I shall not travel alone; an Englishman and a Frenchman are coming with me for two or three years; but I shall stay on. Good-bye, Painting, except as an amusement: my house will be one of carved woodwork.

" I have had a letter from Z—, very long and full of his troubles. I am really afraid that in a year's time he may be seriously attacked by hypochondriacal mania. All this is not very cheerful and doesn't at all encourage me to stay on in this filthy Europe."

During his long illness, in a condition in which his ambition was blunted by indifference, Gauguin had thoroughly thought out his position. He had lost his inclination to take up the cudgels against what he looked upon as a bugbear made up of many petty interests, which when brought together and properly organized formed a considerable power, only to be successfully opposed through patience and above all through the ability to recruit allies; and this was not his affair. If he ventured to enter upon

the conflict alone, he would be fighting continually on two fronts, against enemies who were also bitterly opposed to each other and were both sufficiently strong to keep each other at bay. He would only be a shuttlecock between the two parties. This demanded an endurance to which neither his nature nor his strength was equal.

He would retire beneath the palms and try to find peace in himself and wait till life or death overtook him. And he thought he would be able to accomplish this if only he could settle accounts once for all with his past and with that part of his ego which was still floundering in its net. It was here that the enemy lurked; the question was: could he overcome it? He would make the attempt.

When he came back to his studio and saw it stripped of almost everything of value, his feelings were only reflected in a contemptuous shrug of the shoulders. So at any rate Annah was out of the story. No female domestic should ever come here again. His youthful admirer, the seventeen-year-old sculptor Paco Durio, whom he intended to take with him on his voyage, was a capable and active housekeeper and desired nothing better than to be in the master's company.

It was not long before the circle reassembled in the rue Vercingétorix, and there were a few new faces among them. Of these August Strindberg particularly interested Gauguin. The Swedish writer's

fanatical absorption in all manner of subjects, his violent alternations between the most savage misanthropy and tender humanitarianism, his fits of frankness and taciturnity, appealed to Gauguin. He saw that in his own way Strindberg was at war with civilization — was lonely and afraid of being alone. He guessed that in many ways he had an opponent in this man, but an altogether worthy opponent, whom he felt he could outstrip in his struggle with civilized society.

Every means was resorted to in order to make the sale of his pictures an event, and so Gauguin asked Strindberg, who wrote beautiful French, to contribute the preface to the catalogue; but Strindberg declined in a long letter.

" You insist upon having the preface to your catalogue written by me, in memory of the winter of 1894–5, which we are spending here behind the Institut, not far from the Panthéon, nearest of all to the cemetery of Montparnasse.

" I should have been glad to let you have this souvenir to take with you to that island of Oceania where you are going in search of a setting in harmony with and spacious enough for your mighty stature, but I find myself at the very start in an equivocal position and I hasten to reply to your request by an ' I cannot,' or, more brutally, by an ' I will not.'

" At the same time I owe you an explanation of
my refusal, which does not arise from any unfriend-
liness or from a lazy pen, although I might easily
have thrown the blame on the state of my hands,
which, by the way, has not yet put a stop to my
working.

" Here you have it: I cannot get hold of your art
and I cannot like it. (I have no grasp of your art,
which this time is exclusively Tahitian.) But I
know that this admission will neither surprise nor
wound you, for it appears to me that the hatred of
others does nothing but strengthen you: your personality relishes the antipathy it excites, in its anxiety to remain intact.

" And perhaps you are right there, for as soon as
you were approved and admired, you would have a
band of followers, you would be classified and la-
belled, your art would be given a name which in less
than five years the younger generation would use to
brand a superannuated art, doing their utmost to
hasten its decease.

" I myself have made serious efforts to classify
you, to bring you in as a link in the chain, to trace the
historical connections of your development, but in
vain.

" I remember my first stay in Paris, in 1876. The
town was gloomy, for the nation was in mourning
for the events that had happened and uneasy about
the future; there was ferment in the air.

" In Swedish artistic circles the name of Zola had not yet been heard, for *L'Assommoir* had not been published; I was present at the performance of *Rome vaincue* at the Théâtre Français, when Madame Sarah Bernhardt, the new star, was crowned as a second Rachel, and my young artist friends had dragged me to Durand-Ruel's to see something altogether new in painting. A young painter, then unknown, took me round, and we saw some very marvellous canvases, most of them signed Manet or Monet. But as I had other things to do in Paris besides looking at pictures (as secretary of the Library of Stockholm I had to search for an old Swedish missal in the Library of Sainte-Geneviève), I regarded this new painting with placid indifference. But next day I came back, without really knowing why, and I discovered a ' something ' in these odd manifestations. I saw the pushing of a crowd on a steamer gangway, but I did not see the crowd itself; I saw the speed of an express train in a Normandy landscape, the movement of wheels in the street, hideous portraits of ugly people who could not sit still. Struck by these extraordinary canvases, I sent an article to a paper at home in which I attempted a translation of the sensations I believed the Impressionists had tried to express; and my article had a certain success, being taken as incomprehensible.

" When I returned to Paris for the second time, in 1883, Manet was dead, but his spirit was alive in

a whole school which disputed hegemony with Bastien Lepage; during my third stay in Paris, in 1885, I saw the exhibition of Manet's works. By that time the movement had gained a foothold; it had produced its effect and was now classified. In the *Exposition triennale*, same year, complete anarchy. Every kind of style, colour, and subject: historical, mythological, and naturalistic. Nobody would hear another word of schools or tendencies. Liberty was now the watchword. Taine had said that beauty was not prettiness, and Zola that art was a segment of nature seen through the medium of a temperament.

" Nevertheless, in the midst of the dying convulsions of Naturalism, one name was pronounced with universal admiration, that of Puvis de Chavannes. There he was, quite alone, like a contradiction, painting with the soul of a believer, while not entirely neglecting his contemporaries' taste for allusion. (The term ' Symbolism ' had not yet been invented, a very unfortunate designation for a thing so old as allegory.)

" It was towards Puvis de Chavannes that my thoughts travelled yesterday evening, when, to the southern sounds of mandolin and guitar, I saw on the walls of your studio that confusion of sun-drenched pictures by which I have been haunted in my sleep last night. I saw trees that no botanist could put a name to, animals whose existence Cuvier never suspected, and men whom only you could have created.

A sea which looked like a lava-flow, a sky that no God would find habitable.

" ' Monsieur,' I said in my dream, ' you have created a new heaven and a new earth, but I don't feel comfortable in the midst of your creation: your sunshine is too strong for me, I prefer the effect of light and shade. And your paradise is the home of an Eve who is not my ideal; for I, too, actually have a womanly ideal, or more than one! '

" This morning I paid a visit to the Luxembourg to glance at Chavannes, who kept recurring to my mind. I contemplated with deep sympathy the poor fisherman, so entirely taken up with the catch which is to bring him the faithful love of his wife, who is picking flowers, and of his idle child. That is beautiful! But here I am, confronted with the crown of thorns — and that is a thing I hate, monsieur, I would have you to know that! I will have nothing to do with this pitiful God who turns the other cheek. No, no, give me rather Vitzliputzli devouring human hearts in the sunshine.

" No, Gauguin was not made from a rib of Chavannes, nor from one of Manet or Bastien Lepage either!

" What is he, then? He is Gauguin, the savage who hates the constraint of civilization, something like a Titan, jealous of the Creator, who in his spare time makes a little creation of his own; a child who takes his toys to pieces and uses them to make others,

one who rejects and defies, preferring to see the sky red rather than blue with the crowd.

" Upon my word, I believe that writing this has warmed me so that I am beginning to have a certain understanding of Gauguin's art.

" A modern author has been blamed for not drawing real beings, but just simply inventing his personages himself. Just simply!

" *Bon voyage, Maître;* only, come back to us and to me. By that time perhaps I shall have learned to understand your art better, and that will enable me to write a real preface for a new catalogue in a new Hôtel Drouot; for I, too, am beginning to feel an immense need of turning savage and of creating a new world.

" *August Strindberg* "

Gauguin was moved when he read this letter. Here was a man, a powerful and remarkable personality, who was himself trying to get to the bottom of his own nature and who faced his work with the effort, reluctant but frank and direct, to penetrate his individuality. It encouraged him to trust in the public and to believe that the natural human eye had not yet lost its power of seeing and, through seeing, of understanding at last. This should be the preface to his catalogue and he himself would stretch out a hand to draw them all nearer to him.

" I received your letter today; it is a preface to

my catalogue. I had the idea of asking you for this preface when I saw you the other day in my studio, playing the guitar and singing to it. Your blue eyes — the eyes of a Northerner — examined with attention the pictures hanging on the wall. I had a sense of a revolution, an actual clash between your civilization and my barbarism. The civilization under which you are suffering. The barbarism which to me is a rejuvenation.

" In the presence of the Eve I have chosen, whom I have painted in the forms and harmonies of another world, your memories of your own choice have perhaps conjured up a painful past. The Eve who has her origin in your civilization makes a woman-hater of you, and of nearly all of us.

" The Eve who gave you a fright in my studio will one day make you smile less bitterly. The world which perhaps neither Cuvier nor a botanist would be able to recognize will be a paradise which I have only sketched. And from the sketch to the realization of the dream is a long way. But is it not so that the foreseeing of happiness is a foretaste of Nirvana?

" The Eve I have painted, and she alone, can appear before us naked. Your Eve in this simple costume would not be able to avoid a feeling of shame and would perhaps be too beautiful; she would evoke in us evil, and sorrow.

" In order to make my meaning clearer I will compare not merely these two women but also the

Maori language, a Ural tongue, spoken by my Eve, with the language your woman talks — a language selected from all others, a flexible language, European.

" In the languages of Oceania, when they are in their own element, preserved in their native grossness and free from careful polishing, everything is bare, striking, and primitive, whereas in the inflective languages the roots from which, like all languages, they originated have disappeared in daily use, which has worn away their reliefs and contours. They are like an improved mosaic in which one has ceased to distinguish the joins between the stones, more or less roughly put together, and can no longer admire the work as a handsome lapidary picture. Only a practised eye can follow the construction.

" Excuse this long philological discussion. I think it is necessary for the explanation of the barbaric drawing I have adopted in order to represent pictorially a Ural country and its people.

" Now in conclusion — thanks, Strindberg. When shall we meet again? "

As Gauguin lay on his sick-bed in Brittany he had made up his mind to sell everything that belonged to the past for what it would fetch. So violent had been the shock that nothing seemed to matter but peace. He soon saw that this broken leg was going to be a serious business. He had never had any severe

illness, so the fact of his physical disability made an end of his natural resolution, which had always led him to make plans for the future; now all he cared about was to wind up his affairs and get away.

But when all arrangements had been made for the auction, he began to take a rather different view. The sympathy of his little faithful circle, and especially of Strindberg, gave him encouragement. Certain of his friends — Daniel in particular, on whom he most depended — insisted that he ought to wait awhile and see how things were going. All this restored his feeling of optimism. His business sense was revived: he would not sell without reserve, exposing himself to the speculation of the dealers. On the contrary, he would send prices up at the auction by getting some of his friends to bid on his account. The papers should be worked with announcements of his departure for Tahiti. That had acted as a stimulant on the last occasion, so that his pictures from Brittany now fetched quite good prices. Even in Denmark, Mette had managed to sell some pictures well. Once more he was in full activity, forgetting the pains in his legs and his abominable lameness. He wrote to his wife giving a glowing account of his prospects and suggesting that she should try to sell one or two pictures to a woman friend who had bought before, and then come and visit him, or possibly he would go to Copenhagen.

Everything had been done to make the auction of

February 18th a success. He had forty-nine pictures, drawings, and wood-carvings.

The sale was a terrible disappointment; only a few pictures were really sold, among them two to Degas. There was no life in the bidding; the picture he thought most of, *Manao Tupapau*, only reached nine hundred francs — and that was his own final bid. For *I raro te oviri*, the view from his hut with the two women under the pandanus-trees and the green surf of the Pacific breaking on the sunlit golden sand, it was impossible to get anyone to bid seriously.

The reaction was dreadful; coupled with disappointment at his niggardly lot was bitterness at his own stupidity. Here he sat, a suffering wreck, in his cold, empty studio, watching the golden dream of which he had made a reality being stacked up against the walls, canvases in frames. Oh, what a cheap thing art may become in a moment for him who has sacrificed his life to its creation! One can rid oneself of its burden, others will take that up. But the burden of life? Conscience, injustice done to others, and their injustice to oneself due to misunderstanding and want of understanding, unsatisfied longings for friendship and affection due to want of kindliness, the egoism that results from an absence of the conditions that might make one generous — could all these be put into a sack and abandoned together with the heap of ruins that lay before him?

" *Dear Mette,*

" Your letter! I have been waiting for it a long time. I know what the papers say about me. As long ago as five years you believed in the correctness of the figures *in spite of* what I told you. This time it is another story.

" I fought hard to get my pictures quoted and I spread the rumour of an early departure to give them a value as scarcities. Here are the actual figures.

" The sale fetched   23,640 fr.

" Excepting 1,370 fr. of real sales, everything was *bought in* by me under borrowed names.

7% on 23,640 makes	1,654.80
Hire of room	150.00
Transport	30.00
	1,834.80
Less	1,370.00
	464.80

" As profit I have 464.80 out of my own pocket!!

" Now let us have a little talk. You must admit that since my return any man in my place would have made sorrowful reflections on life, on the family, and all the rest.

" 1. Written by you: ' You will have to get on *by yourself.*'

" 2. Written by the children: Nothing.

" 3. My leg has been broken and it ruins my health. Not a word from my family.

" 4. The winter has been terribly long and I have had no one but myself to take care of my chest, *uselessly*, *chronic* bronchitis. I literally cannot live without sunshine.

" In these conditions, with the *enemies* my painting has made me, I have to take every precaution if I am not to come to grief. *At the age of 47* I WILL not be reduced to poverty, and yet I am very near it; and once down, there is *nobody* in the world who will help me up again. Your words: You will have to get on by yourself, are significant. I take them to heart."

Did Mette ever fully understand what it meant to get on by himself? Had she any thought beyond the purely practical one, that she was looking after herself and their five children? No doubt she had not. How far apart were their ideas! — a deep gulf kept them from coming to an understanding.

To put the blame on her was just as ineffectual as taking it all on himself. But it was he alone who bore the burden of ignominy.

To begin with, the only way of getting rid of it was to go away, back to Tahiti, and continue his work. For this he had to raise funds; by depositing his pictures with a couple of dealers and some interested private persons he succeeded in getting together the money for his voyage and a little capital for making a start in Tahiti. The pictures were to be sold as occasion arose and he was to have monthly

payments sent to Tahiti and a full account of the prices the pictures fetched, whenever one of them was sold. In case of difficulty Daniel de Monfreid held his power of attorney.

If all the promises made to him were kept, his life was more or less secured for the next three years, with reasonable care. His experience with the Breton pictures encouraged him to hope that he would be able to obtain decent prices for the older Tahiti works within that time. And then the picture dealers would approach him. One or two had already appeared on the horizon, like hyenas waiting for their prey to drop; they were beginning to scent him after all. If he could once get his foot in with one of them, the rest would come about of itself. Then one could begin to make plans for the future.

But now the only thing to do was to get away as quietly as possible; no dinners and speeches. A little farewell party at a café for his best friends, where he could appear in his best humour and distribute some drawings among them as a souvenir of the man who was going back to Tahiti to be happy. That was what they must think — and that he would stay there for good. It was to be no *Au revoir*, but a " Forget me not."

He parted from them at the door of the café.

Remember — no seeing-off at the station tomorrow.

Alone he walked towards home, rather unsteadily,

partly on account of his leg. A cab came up alongside and followed him at a walk. He dismissed it with a friendly wave of the hand: " Thanks, I'll walk home the last night I'm here." A streetwalker approached, with her best smile. " What's your name? " — " Henriette." — " And mine's Henri. Will you go home with me? " — " Are you kind? " — " Yes! I'm kind."

Always the same here in Europe, in big things as in small. Buying and selling.

CHAPTER 7

In spite of the unusual calmness of the voyage to Tahiti, Gauguin felt unwell on arriving at Papeete. It was not only the wound in his leg that gave him trouble; he felt slack and had pains in the back of his head — indisposed in a way he had never experienced before. Perhaps his last Parisian adventure with Henriette, casual as it had been, might have a significance that he did not look for. It was no use thinking of that now. He had to see about a house.

This time he chose to settle on the western side of the island, at Pounoaouia, where he rented a site upon which he could build a studio according to his own ideas. His present plan was to lay more stress on monumental decorative composition, avoiding as far as possible all that had to do with the surroundings. The important thing now was to have a large room where he could work with plenty of light.

Even here in Tahiti he would try to break as far as he could with his past and arrive at another frame

of mind, which might bring about a revival in his art. Here on the western side the landscape was bolder in its outlines and more wooded — and the light was different, with more violent transitions between heat and cold.

As the place was at some distance from Papeete, Gauguin was always on the move while the hut was being built, without any fixed place of abode. His whole attention was directed to getting a roof over his head, so that he might settle down to work as soon as possible. He was nervous and restless and tried to shorten the period of waiting by distractions which were not beneficial to his health. All this hurrying backwards and forwards wore him out, now that he had lost his former activity; his lameness troubled him not only physically but morally, since he had always been proud of his powers of endurance and bodily strength.

And when the studio was finished, the next thing was to furnish it according to his taste and to have everything settled so that he could begin work with a feeling of security. All this took time, and autumn was far advanced before he could set to work in earnest. It was a comfort to know that in this climate he could face the winter calmly, contenting himself with regarding it as a picturesque idea which seemed distant and fantastic in these surroundings. But perhaps he would try tuning his palette in simple harmonies and begin with a snow-covered landscape

from Brittany. There was a simplification in it which appealed to him, and which, in another way, he would now try to introduce into his painting.

Always so many things to be thought out before one can begin in earnest.

" *My dear Daniel,*

" At the time of receiving your kind letter I haven't touched a paint-brush, except to do a window in my studio. I had to find temporary quarters in Papeete while making up my mind; finally I decided to build a big Tahitian hut out in the country. The situation is magnificent, I can tell you: in the shade, close to the road, and behind me a view of the mountains that would take your breath away. Imagine a huge birdcage of bamboo lattice-work with a thatched roof of coco palm, divided into two parts by the curtains of my former studio. One of these parts is the bedroom, with very little light, to keep it cool. The other part is the studio, with a big window high up. On the floor, mats and my old Persian carpet; the whole place decorated with hangings, knick-knacks, and drawings.

" As you see, I am not much to be pitied at the moment.

" Every night my bed is invaded by a lot of mad tomboys; there were three of them on duty last night. I'm going to give up this rackety life and take a steady-going woman into the house; then I shall

work like a horse, all the more as I feel in the vein and believe I shall do better work than before.

" My former wife has got married while I was away and I've been obliged to make her husband a cuckold; but she can't come and live with me, in spite of a week's escapade.

" That is the obverse of the medal; the reverse is not so reassuring. As usual when I feel I am in funds and have expectations, I spend freely, trusting in the future and in my talent; then I soon find myself at the end of my tether. When my house is paid for I shall have 900 francs left and I hear *no* news from France, which makes me rather anxious. When I left, Lévy was to send me 2,600 francs owing to me by the Café des Variétés. With other creditors I am owed all together 4,300 francs; I don't receive *even a letter.*

" As always, you are the first to think of me and I am very grateful to you. On receipt of this go and see Lévy, rue Saint-Lazare 57, and tell him I am very uneasy both about my money and about the pictures I left with him. If you are in London, write to Mollard.

" People will say to me: ' Why do you go so far away? ' — But when I go no farther off than Brittany, for instance, it is the same story.

" Listen to what I've done with my family: I've given them the slip. Let my family get out of the mess for themselves, it's not as if I was the only one

to help them!!! I count on spending the rest of my days here in my hut, in perfect peace. — Oh yes, I'm a *great criminal*. What does it matter! Michelangelo was another; and I am not Michelangelo."

When once Gauguin made a start he worked with a violent effort and did not spare himself. His thoughts were fixed on the present moment, on the experience that had inspired his work, often with an intensity and an absorption that continually enhanced the dramatic conflict between himself as a European and the people he loved. Whenever he tried to simplify his way of thinking, by forgetting the distance separating their natural candour and instinctive manifestation of beauty from his own passionate and conscious interest in their beauty, he had a guilty feeling of intruding upon their mystic spiritual life, with which he was really unqualified to identify himself. He enjoyed them, delighted in them; and it gave him a voluptuous feeling to reproduce their beauty. Nevertheless the relation between him and them remained that of the wolf and its prey, and he was constantly reminded that the natives of Tahiti, owing to the countless outrages they had suffered at the hands of Europeans, themselves had an instinctive sense of this, although they approached the wolf without fear and put themselves in his power. Because they had not yet learned the meaning of fear.

Gauguin gave way to this feeling, at the very time when he longed more than ever to put his whole civilized past behind him and adopt the life of these beautiful creatures. Would he succeed in this or would his memories continue to overwhelm him and mingle with the pain of his sleepless nights?

Would he never escape from the clutches of art or of his dependence on civilization, so that all he could depict was an ever elusive experience, beautiful and tragic? The mere image of it was enough to make him forget for a moment that the God of his race had once driven his race out of this paradise, and that he alone could never return to it.

Now that he stood on the threshold of paradise, civilization called him back. Money difficulties from the Old World were lying in wait for him. The malady he brought from thence insidiously gained ground. The letters he received from his wife were brief and contained only practical questions, most of them difficult of solution. She on her side was hurt by his failure to understand her position, and she had nothing to reproach herself with, having followed the letter of the law in which she had been brought up.

He was menaced on every side and his power of resistance was paralysed. Sickness found him an easy prey.

" The accident I had here in Tahiti was nearly fatal; as a result of privations and agitations my heart

was in a very bad state and it was difficult to stop the vomiting of blood. According to the doctor a relapse would be the end of me, and in future I must take precautions.

" So in future if you have any more letters to write me like those I have recently received, I would ask you not to do so. My work is not finished and I must go on living.

" Think this over. And stop these everlasting lamentations which do no good and a lot of harm. I might reply to you (that is, if you had an understanding heart except for your children): Do you think I am lying on a bed of roses?

" Could you possibly send me my pair of swords? I might have a use for them some day."

His prospects on leaving the hospital were not bright. Everything seemed to fail him, when in his enfeebled state he needed the fulfilment of all bargains.

" *My dear Daniel*,

" A few words in haste to catch the mail. I am in hospital worn out with suffering and I hope to be cured in a month's time, but how am I going to pay the hospital? Last month you and Z— announced that money was on the way. A mistake: Mauffra made excuses; heavy unforeseen expenses prevented his carrying out his engagement, but in the following month the money should reach me without fail. This

month neither money nor a letter from anybody.

" I write to you because there is an officer going to France, taking with him some canvases of mine, rather dauby on account of my state of health; and then I have a temperament which drives me to finish a picture straight away while the fever lasts. Whereas working only one hour a day . . .

" However, such as they are, I send them to you. Perhaps they are good; I have put into them so much anguish, so much suffering, that this may compensate for the clumsy execution. Mauclair says I am revolting in my grossness and brutality. — What an injustice — "

By degrees Gauguin became as though possessed by all this waiting and by an infinite loathing of having to write the same letters again and again. The little strength his illness left him for working was used up on this spectre of waiting, and whenever news came it was as before — nothing! And then, what he always felt was the worst of all, having to go cap in hand to borrow money for bare necessities and the expenses entailed by his illness. For two years he was occupied with little else. Many a time when his illness was at its worst, he hoped it might make an end of him. Broadly speaking, he had nothing more to live for, if he could not get to work. Far away on the horizon of his thoughts he had a glimpse of some children he loved, and especially a daughter. He took

out the little booklet he wrote for her when he was last in Tahiti, in which he told her who her father was and what were his thoughts. In it was a little water-colour sketch of his picture *Manao Tupapau* — the spirit of the departed watching over the little naked girl who is lying in her bed and staring into the darkness. The spirit raises its hand to admonish and protect.

" To my daughter Aline this little book is dedicated. Scattered notes, disconnected like dreams, like life itself, all made up of fragments."

She is to have this after his death. He turns the pages and begins to read:

" Woman's nature is love, but it is this love that conceives, and in conception she abandons herself unconditionally. Woman only attains her full individuality in abandoning herself. Woman desires to be free and has a right to be free. And truly it is not man who hinders her.

" On the day when her honour is no longer seated under the navel, she will be set free, and perhaps her health will be improved."

" We are told that God took a lump of clay and made all that you know. The artist for his part ought not to copy nature, if he really wishes to create a divine masterpiece, but should take elements from nature and from them create a new element.

" There is something of this in the words: Increase and multiply. To increase is to be strong.

Multiply: Increase the created by a new creation.

" A true painter always feels a certain shame in borrowing another's beauty. It is not the subject, but his work, that ought to be beautiful."

" In the firmament there is a book in which are written the laws of harmony and beauty. The men who know how to read this book, says Swedenborg, are the favoured of God. And he adds that the artist is the true elect, since he alone has the power to write this book, and he must be looked upon as God's messenger."

" I have known perfect misery. I have suffered hunger and cold and all they bring in their train; one grows accustomed to this, and with some strength of will one ends by laughing at it. But it is terrible to be hindered in one's work.

" In Paris especially, as in all great cities, the hunt for money takes up three-quarters of one's time and half one's energy.

" It is quite true that suffering whets the edge of genius. But there must not be too much of it. For then it kills you.

" With a good share of arrogance I have succeeded in acquiring much energy, and I have trained myself to will.

" Is arrogance a fault and ought one to develop it? I say yes! It is once for all the best way of fighting against the human beast that dwells in us."

Perhaps, like himself, Aline has had it dinned into

her ears that he is a man who has deserted his wife and children.

Well, that is true enough, but has she been told why?

" Is it not something of a miscalculation that everything is to be sacrificed to the children? And does not this mean depriving the nation of the creative ability of its most efficient members?

" You sacrifice yourself for your child, as he will sacrifice himself in turn when he grows up. And so it goes on. There will be nothing left but sacrifice. And cowardice will be long-lasting."

He puts the little book back in the drawer, takes up her photograph, and examines it. The fine, strong lines of her profile, the heavy eyelids, the high and narrow shape of the head, and the rather melancholy look about the mouth are cast in the same mould as his own, only less affected by the storms of time. She is so like him. In her disposition too, no doubt, as he understands from Mette's letters. To her he can write all this, which she will understand when she is grown up. She was only thirteen when this portrait was taken, but now she is twenty. He himself is nearly fifty, and finished. The book will soon be hers.

Aline was now the strongest tie which bound him to his family. One day it was brutally severed. His wife informed him that Aline had died of pneumonia; the winter had been too severe for her. She

now lay buried far away under the cold white snow.

" I read over the shoulder of a friend who is writing: ' I have just lost my daughter. I no longer love God. She was called Aline, after my mother —

" ' Everyone loves in his own way: with some love surges up over the coffin; with others . . . I don't know.

" ' Her grave far away, the flowers — an empty show, all this.

" ' Her grave is here, close beside me. My tears are the flowers upon it — living flowers these.' "

The news of Aline's death reached him at a time when one misfortune after another was crowding upon him.

" Every day, as thoughts press upon me, the wound grows deeper and at this moment I have lost heart altogether. I must certainly have an enemy somewhere up above who will not allow me a minute's peace.

" The man from whom I leased a little patch of ground to build my hut on has just died, leaving his affairs in great disorder, and in consequence his land has been sold. So now I am looking for a bit of ground and I shall have to rebuild.

" I have received *Les Hommes du jour* (sent by Schuffenecker, with an absurd portrait of me, done by him). This fellow makes me tired; what an idiot! And what pretension! A cross, some flames, and there you are! That's symbolism —

" I'm trying to amuse myself with wood-engraving, any wood I can get hold of and no press. . . .

" I have managed at last to get a loan of 1,000 francs for one year out of the Caisse Agricole (the bank of Tahiti). With this I have bought a plot for 700 francs (too big for me, but the only one to be had) near where I am living (about a hundred yards). With the remaining 300 francs I shall rebuild and refurnish. I have still 200 francs in cash to live on. Later on I shall recover the price of my purchase, seeing that there are a hundred coconut palms on this piece of land which may bring me in 500 francs a year. If my health permits and if I have a few sous left to spend, I shall plant vanilla there; it pays well and doesn't require much labour. Who knows! perhaps some day I may find myself free and with nothing to worry about."

Gauguin's brain was continually occupied with economic visions. Especially at night he would drive away evil thoughts by building castles in the air and thus obtain a few hours of peaceful sleep, in which his fancies lived on in his dreams and often assumed marvellous shapes. Then the daylight brought him back to a reality which sometimes made him think of taking his own life and thus entering on the sleep of which he was so badly in need. But as often as not he was tormented by nightmares, and then the days were more endurable. The landscape was spread out before him in all its beauty. Nature herself was there,

so strangely untouched by all the misfortunes that lie in wait for one everywhere. There was something eternally constant about this nature, which rose again, as proud and as young as ever, after the raging of the elements. What curious beings men were, after all, how fleeting and inconstant — beginning as nothing and ending as nothing, racking their brains through life in the effort to understand their own nature and the mystery of life, without ever getting to the bottom of these questions: Whence do we come? Who are we? And whither are we going? But while we are alive we are a part of nature, an element in that which gives it a beauty. A beauty which in one way or another we feel constrained to express.

Gauguin had made up his mind to die, but before that he would paint a great picture which was to sum up all that he had experienced in his passage through life.

" I assure you I had resolved to die last December. But before dying I wished to paint a great picture which was in my head, and for that whole month I worked at it night and day in a tremendous fever. I can tell you, it isn't a picture like Puvis de Chavannes's, with studies from nature, preliminary cartoons, and all the rest of it. The whole thing is done offhand, with a coarse brush, on a piece of sacking full of knots and wrinkles, so its appearance is terribly rough.

" They will say it has been left unfinished. It is

true that one is not a good judge of one's own work, but, all the same, I believe not only that this canvas is better than all that have gone before, but in fact that I shall never do anything better or approaching it. Before dying I have put into it all my energy, so much passionate pain and a vision so clear that it needs no correction and conceals the hastiness of the work, bringing it all to life. This does not stink of the model, the craft, and the alleged rules — from which I have always emancipated myself, though sometimes with apprehension.

" It is a canvas measuring fourteen feet nine inches by five and a half feet in height. The two upper corners are chrome yellow, with the inscription on the left and my signature on the right, like a fresco damaged at the corners and applied on a golden wall. Below on the right a baby asleep, then three women squatting on the ground. Two figures dressed in purple are confiding their reflections to each other; a figure, purposely drawn huge in spite of perspective, raises its arms and looks with astonishment at these two personages who dare to think of their destiny. A figure in the centre is plucking fruit. Two cats beside a child. A white goat. The idol, raising its two arms mysteriously and rhythmically, seems to foreshadow the future state. A seated figure appears to be listening to the idol; then an old woman near to death seems to accept it, resigning herself to her thoughts, and she brings the legend to an end; at her

feet a strange bird, holding a lizard in its claws, represents the futility of empty words. The scene is by a stream in the woods. In the background the sea, then the mountains of the neighbouring island. In spite of the transitions of tone the aspect of the landscape from one end to the other is blue and Veronese green. From this all the nude figures stand out in a bold orange. Supposing one were to say to the pupils of the Beaux-Arts competing for the prix de Rome: 'The picture that you have to paint is to represent: " Whence do we come? Who are we? Whither are we going? " ' — what would they make of it? I have finished a philosophical work on this theme compared with the Gospel; I think it's good. If I feel strong enough to copy it out, I will send it to you."

After the picture had reached a point at which he was able to make up his mind about it, he seemed to awaken to new life. He felt that he was not yet at the end of his powers and energy; he still had something to say. That what was intended to be a conclusion had in reality opened a way for him to a yet greater liberation and increased decorative and monumental simplicity. He sat studying it day after day. The picture came to life and repeated the words of Pascal. When does a picture begin and when is it finished? Can a real work of art ever be so perfected as to contain the whole soul of the artist? Or will there not be a vacuum somewhere which he will wish to fill up —

especially in painting, which lives entirely in a world of its own, unrelated to surrounding space?

It is in this vacuum that new ideas develop, trying to create a new world in which the soul of the artist may lose itself anew.

His pictorial imagination was set in motion and again sought to control his ideas. Life was worth while, after all, even if things looked almost hopeless.

Before very long he would have to repay the loan from the bank, otherwise it would distrain on his house and the many canvases he had deposited as security. And even if he could postpone a settlement by paying an instalment, it would be the same thing in six months' time. And he had to live, and above all to get well. His head was buzzing with schemes; he wrote home, peremptorily demanding what was due to him, proposing to turn himself into a sort of corporation, describing his position in the blackest colours, making appeals both to pity and to common sense. In short, he wished to live. But at home everything took time; the driblets that reached him barely covered his first instalment to the bank. In order to live he had to accept the most ordinary office employment at six francs a day. Good-bye to painting for a while. And then he had to move to Papeete, the most dangerous place for a European; but it had to be done, while waiting for the wheel to turn. Little

straws told him that the wind was about to change
in his favour. A new and very remarkable picture
dealer, Ambroise Vollard, who specialized in Cézanne, seemed to have taken a fancy to him. But he
knew the importance of not being in too great a
hurry. As usual he explained all this at length to his
friend Daniel, and asked him to see Degas. His old
resolution was awakened, he shrank from nothing
which might help him to get back to his hut and his
work. And he descried a faint hope of being able to
return to France, when once he had fully worked out
the idea that had been fostered by his great picture.

Living in the town was disastrous to Gauguin. He
could not work at his art, and intercourse with the
Europeans very rarely had a good influence on his
character. His rather outspoken utterances on every
subject except art did not fall on good ground, and
this was particularly true of his political views,
which were far too much influenced by his indignation against the French colonial administration.
The contemptuous way in which the Europeans
treated the natives scandalized him so that he whole-
heartedly took the part of the latter; and very soon
he came to be looked upon as an oddity, a man
whom one stood drinks to make him talk and have a
good laugh at his expense. His direct insults were
ignored. If he had had his duelling swords there
would have been no opportunity of using them. With
one or two exceptions the other colonists were inca-

pable of understanding him as an artist, and as a man they were inclined to despise him, particularly as he was an artist without apparent means of existence. The effect of all this was that his malady, which had shown some improvement, again got the upper hand, so that he had to return to the hospital. And, as things were, this meant utter ruin.

Then it was that the wheel of fortune began very slowly to move in the right direction. Some of his pictures had been sold in France, and at the close of '98 he received word that Vollard offered to buy and he sent him nine canvases. At the beginning of the new year he was able to move back to his hut and resume his old life with his young *vahiné*, who would soon bear him a child.

Everything now looked really brighter, but unfortunately it took him several months to obtain some relief from the eczema which had taken a disquieting turn during his stay at Papeete and still kept him awake at night. At the same time he was worried by the thought of his compatriots in the town and their treatment of him, and of how he could shake things up in the colony.

He hit upon the unhappy idea, in association with an ex-sailor, now a merchant in a large way and a political malcontent, of starting a paper, *Les Guêpes*, which would give him an outlet for his indignation against the administration of the island and against the priesthood.

" Enclosed a bit of a paper which will tell you about the rumpus I raised last month. Result: nothing against me, neither duel nor prosecution. What a rotten state of affairs in our colonies! Anyhow it was time to do something of this sort, because everybody was inclined to tread on my toes, taking me to be a man without a penny. Today they are beginning to show, if not respect, at least a salutary fear."

As usual, he acted openly and accepted the whole responsibility — as well as all the work of providing the paper with illustrations and of printing it, which was done with a hectograph.

No notice at all was taken of the paper and there was not much chance of its having any circulation to speak of. This only spurred Gauguin on, and his impetuous temperament, which had been rendered extremely nervous by the sufferings of the last few years, became so excessively occupied with this that he started another paper on his own account — *Le Sourire* — with the same make-up, but rather more elaborate and illustrated with woodcuts. He was so busy with this that he entirely forgot that his affairs were looking up. It had become a matter of life and death for him to clear away all the corruption he thought he could see in these colonies. And the less attention was paid to his attacks, the greater was his disgust with it all, entirely darkening his view of the beautiful island. It lost its charm for him, as did also the natives, who in the years that had passed since

PHOTO, DRUET, PARIS

PORTRAIT OF HIMSELF
1898

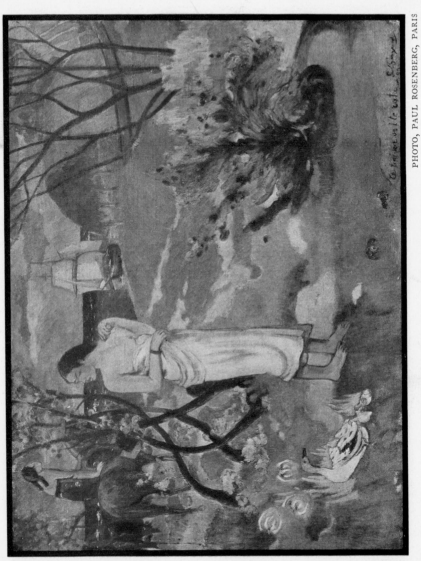

THE SAILOR'S DREAM

TAHITI, 1899

his former visit had become more and more marked by European influence. He noticed in many little things how hypocrisy was slowly but surely gaining ground everywhere among the natives, so that the illusion he had tried to keep up, that they were only guided by natural instincts, was destroyed by many little incidents. All this made a deep impression on him. His own character had changed and become irritable, so that he treated his *vahiné* in a way that could only lead him to reproach himself. He, too, had become a ruffian, a bandit, everything he would hate to be, in the eyes of these people. And just at this time when he needed more than ever to work out his idea of the primitive, the simple, and the natural — and when, to all appearances, he might have found peace to do so. Now he was once more a homeless vagrant, and, what made it worse, ill, injured, and lame.

His desire of following out his idea was further intensified by the reception given to his last things in France, and particularly the big picture he had sent home. Even Daniel expressed himself rather vaguely about it — confining himself for the most part to strictures on its awkward shape, the coarse canvas and faulty preparation. All this showed that he was on the right course. He pursued his aim by following the flight of his thought. That which the others had seen in his previous Tahiti pictures, and which he himself had never intended to express, he would now

sweep away with his new pictures. The symbolism which Charles Morice, for instance, had inserted in *Noa-Noa*, with his Reminiscences, Fancies, and Dreams, was foreign to anything he had had in mind. He would take that book up, too, and purify it of all the vague and obscure sentiment that was so entirely opposed to his nature.

The task he had undertaken was not concluded, an immense work lay before him and he had to perform it. But how would that be possible here, in an atmosphere infected by the foul breath of the Europeans — where he himself was poisoned day by day by his own malicious thoughts of his compatriots? His relations with his *vahiné* and his child had gradually assumed the form of a distant memory, a connubial life which he believed to be forgotten. They were dominated by the necessity of keeping a strict watch on the uncontrollable element in his own temper, by a feeling of impotence in not being able to give free rein to his nature, a sense of dependence which was heightened more and more by his conscience.

He had to get away, to recover his powers, together with peace and freedom; and again he recalled his friend the captain's description of the Marquesas Islands — that still unspoilt group in the midst of the ocean, and among them Hiva-oa with its mighty mountain on which the wild goats leapt, with its long, fertile valleys where the bird-life was

as teeming as the wild bananas, and where shoals of
fish were chased inshore by the whales so that one
could scoop them up in one's hands. And the natives
were handsomer than any other race on earth, proud
and reserved, yet friendly and obliging.

Gauguin had had thoughts of going there before,
and now the longing came on him again. He watched
attentively every boat which drew near the coast
under full sail.

Only when he was there and could begin his work
again would he be able to take advantage of the
rather more favourable breeze which seemed to
reach him from his native land. At any rate his immediate future was assured; what would happen beyond that, time would show. The optimist in him was
not yet buried; he must be brought back to life. The
latest letters from Daniel were of great assistance. A
rich wine-grower, Monsieur Fayet, who painted a
little himself, was showing a great interest in his pictures. When once the private buyers had made their
appearance, he would be able to tighten up his terms
with the picture dealers.

Farewell, Tahiti. A new life was about to begin on
the most beautiful island of the vast Pacific.

CHAPTER 8

THE Marquesas Islands lie in the midst of the Pacific, some seven hundred miles from Tahiti; far out of the usual steamer tracks, lonelier than any other group of islands in the great ocean, they rise to a height of four thousand feet in bold and majestic outlines. Until about the middle of last century, when the French annexed them, they had only been visited casually by white men. A strong and handsome Maori race, numbering about ten thousand, was in possession, living as fishermen and hunters and on the fruits which abounded in the wide valleys among the mountains. By this time, forty years or more after the French had taken possession of the island and made it monastic property, the native population had dwindled to barely two thousand souls. Christian morality, which was authoritatively asserted by the Catholic missionaries, had weakened the resistance of these children of nature to their only dangerous enemies, leprosy and syphilis, which the Europeans had brought with them. The women had become

barren and the men had lost their zest as hunters, now that they had to work for a foreign master. Broadly speaking, all property interests were in the hands of the Church; the struggle between civilization and the native population proceeded silently. The vigilance of Christian morality took care that natural instincts were kept in check within the framework of the Catholic Church. Ignorant of its meaning, the natives chanted their Te Deum as an elegy over their own race.

As soon as Gauguin landed at Atuana, the capital, which was situated on the largest island, Hiva-oa, he was shown the reverse side of the country in which he had been longing to find peace and quiet and renewed activity.

" Things had reached such a pitch that I said to myself it was time to make for a simpler country with not so much officialdom. And I thought of packing up and going to the Marquesas, the promised land, where estates, food, and poultry could be had for the asking and where you had a gendarme as gentle as a lamb to show you round.

" Promptly, with an easy mind, innocent as a virgin taking the veil, I embarked and arrived in peace at Atuana, the chief town of Hiva-oa.

" I had to climb down very considerably. The ant is not given to lending, whatever her other faults may be; and I had the look of a grasshopper that had been singing all the summer.

" On arriving I was met with the news that no land was to be leased or sold except by the mission, and even there it was doubtful. The bishop was away and I had to wait a month; my trunks and a whole cargo of building timber were left on the beach.

" During this month, as you may imagine, I went to mass every Sunday, being obliged to play the part of a good Catholic and an enemy of the Protestants. My reputation was made, and Monseigneur, never suspecting my hypocrisy, was kind enough (since it was I) to sell me a little plot covered with pebbles and scrub at the price of 650 francs. I set to work with a will and, thanks again to some men recommended by the bishop, I was quickly housed.

" There is something to be said for hypocrisy.

" When once my hut was finished, I thought no more of fighting the Protestant pastor, who, by the way, is a well-bred young man and very liberal-minded; nor had I any thoughts of returning to the church."

Gauguin's hut was situated close to the high-road and in a fairly populous region, but it was on marshy ground at the bottom of a stony scree and hidden from the road by thick bushes. He had therefore built the hut on strong piles, high enough above the ground to give room underneath for a stable, a cart-shed and a tool-house. A steep and primitive flight of stairs led up to a little veranda in front of the house itself, which measured ten yards by three and a half,

with a sloping roof thatched with palm-leaves. The front wall was of woodwork, but the others were built of perpendicular bamboo canes, so that the breeze could blow through them and the moonbeams could play their *vivo* at night. A large side window provided a good light for the long room. At the back of the house was a little bedroom, just big enough to take a bed, a bedside table, a chair, and a wash-stand. The studio contained only the barest necessities, a table and a couple of chairs, bast mats on the floor, and the indispensable easel. Meals were taken on the veranda.

The eczema had spread; he had difficulty in walking and usually had to ride when he went about. And when the pains in his leg and foot were too severe he drove in a long, low four-wheeled cart he had built, enabling him to sit back with his legs extended.

He had little intercourse with the Europeans, but on the other hand it was not long before he got in touch with the natives.

The very first day after the house was finished, as Gauguin sat on his veranda sunning himself, naked except for the *pareo* about his loins, his neighbour Tioka came up, full of confidence, and offered his help; and Gauguin knew by experience that this help would cost him infinitely less than any he might get from the mission. No claim was made on his gratitude nor was there any interference with his

desire to live in his own way. But at the same time he had no doubt that the intimate relations he wished to establish with the natives would not be looked upon with favour by the ministers of the Church. The first duty of a priest in the colonies is to watch over the virtue of others. But Gauguin was in fighting trim, fully prepared to be a guardian of morality in his own way, as a decided opponent of hypocrisy and its poisonous effect on the healthy and genuine nature of the Maori.

" A hen came to call and that started the war.

" When I say a hen I am speaking modestly; as a matter of fact, all the hens arrived, without any invitation on my part.

" Monseigneur is a buck-rabbit, whereas I am an old cock, pretty tough and fairly well up to the ropes. If I say that the rabbit began it I am speaking the truth. Trying to put me under a vow of chastity! That's a little too strong; can't have any of that, my dear.

" To cut two splendid pieces of rosewood and carve them in the Marquesan fashion was child's play to me. One represented a horned devil (Père Paillard). The other a charming woman, flowers in her hair. It was enough to call her Thérèse for everyone without exception, even the school-children, to see the allusion to this famous love-affair.

" If it's a myth, it was not I who invented it.

" My word, how we gossip here! If ever I return

to Paris I shall be fit to take a place as concierge and read the feuilleton of the *Petit Journal* every morning.

" For that matter, no conversation is possible here except gossiping and obscenities; from the very cradle the children are up to snuff. To tell the truth, it is always the same thing, like one's daily bread.

" It is not always witty, but it gives one a relief after one's work; frivolity of mind and body. The women are venal and make no bones about it. Besides, this gives you an escape from tiresome austerity, and from the ugly hypocrisy which makes people so wicked.

" An orange and a sidelong glance; that's enough.

" The orange of which I am speaking varies from one to two francs; it's hardly worth while denying oneself. One can easily be a little Sardanapalus without going bankrupt.

" No doubt the reader will be asking for the idyll, because you can't have a book without an idyll. But —

" This is not a book. . . .

" I asked the native interpreter: ' My boy, how do you say " an idyll " in the Marquesan language? ' And he replied: ' What a joker you are! ' Pursuing my investigations, I said to him: ' What is your word for " virtue "? ' And the honest fellow answered with a laugh: ' Do you take me for an idiot? '

" The pastor himself says that it's a sin. And the

women, like frightened deer, seem to say with their velvet eyes: ' That's not true.' A Parisienne would say: ' Talk away! '

" I know very well that at home, in Paris or in the provinces, retired officials will tell you strange yarns. Don't believe a word of them; *here* the monsters are natural enough. They see quite well, though without showing it, that our uniform caps are ridiculous and that we are a lot of beasts if we make out they are not.

" They promise, say the women, and they don't keep their promises. In other words, that won't go down.

" Apart from this they snap their fingers at us all the time.

" If you should come across, at the Helder or any other pot-house, a colonial Governor called Ed. Petit, take a good look at him, he's a queer bird.

" Imagine it! when he came to the Marquesas, long ago, as purser of the *Hugon,* he made a good many marriages *à la* Loti, and being proud of one of these wives, he thought he would treat himself to the head of his mother-in-law, who was residing a few feet below the soil in this charming island that they call Taoata.

" They scratched away and disinterred her, and when our purser wanted to carry off the famous head, his father-in-law called out: ' How many piastres? '

" ' It's priceless,' replied our witty purser. No-

body is more obstinate than a father-in-law who demands piastres, and the famous head was restored to its eternal home.

" Like Hop-o'-my-Thumb, our purser inadvertently strewed little pebbles to show the way and at night carried off the coveted head.

" The missionary (a look-out man who misses nothing) made a written complaint to the captain of the *Hugon*, who furiously informed our purser that a mother-in-law was a sacred thing. . . .

" When up for his examination at the École Coloniale, he was given this question: ' How do you set about balancing a budget? '

" Answer: ' That's quite simple, you tear it up.'

" That's your colonizer! . . .

" An American paper informs us that the murdered President Mac Lean [*sic*] died, in the opinion of the physicians, from want of vitality!!

" Here a question of procedure arises. Want of vitality: isn't this a formal inaccuracy? And in that case wouldn't one have a chance of upsetting it in the Court of Cassation?

" This extraordinary Governor whom they call Ed. Petit writes to the Minister: ' In the Marquesas the native race is fast disappearing. Wouldn't it be as well to send us the surplus from Martinique? '

" This was written after the volcanic disaster.

" It reminds one rather of that aide-de-camp who went in search of the Emperor Napoleon I: ' Sire,

a hundred thousand men are waiting for you below. Wouldn't it be as well to bring them up by the little private staircase? ' To which Napoleon I answered: ' Tell them to come in, my good man! '

" If you come across this Ed. Petit, at the Helder or any of those places, or even at the Folies-Bergère, tell him he takes the prize."

The two figures, Père Paillard and Thérèse, adorned the posts of the gate leading from the public road to Gauguin's property. The natives never omitted to show his reverence the respect they had been taught to pay to his person; and now they paid the same respect to his image, the women saluting him with a cordiality which the priest would have preferred to avoid in broad daylight. Gauguin had not been many months in Hiva-oa before the native population of the island quite understood that " Koké " was a man in whom they could confide absolutely without running any risk. And he saw more and more clearly that he ought to protect these handsome and lovable children of nature against the instinct of his own race to exploit them clandestinely while openly degrading them by systematically trying to eradicate the culture to which the Maoris had attained through their natural sense of beauty and entirely natural instincts and impulses. As a race they possessed a beauty of their own, resulting from centuries of intimate association with natural surroundings that made great demands on their physical

adroitness and presence of mind. In return this nature has been generous and has spared them lurking dangers; these people therefore enjoy nature and their own life in it, and their creative imagination has made of it an idol for their adoration. It revolted Gauguin that this should be destroyed by the ruthless belief of his own race in its superiority, without its offering anything of value in return. It revolted him because as an artist he saw something in himself which was reflected in these people's proud and naïve dignity, in their frank and simple nature and lively humanity. And to this was added their plastic beauty, the sure and graceful rhythm of their movements and the expressiveness with which their every mood was shown in their features.

The quiet and stubborn fight the Catholic priesthood carried on against the Maoris was an attack not only on them, but also on the best instincts in himself, in which his art had struck fertile roots. And that was why he took up the fight.

All his life Gauguin's attitude to religious and political opinions had been one of indifference. To his mind it was all a question of the right of the individual to live his own life without being brought into conflict with his own conscience.

The priesthood in the Marquesas regarded such views as anarchical; but their guilty conscience made them dread any outside interference in their isolated existence, which facilitated their arbitrary exercise

of power. They appeared to shut their eyes, but were watching carefully for an opportunity of intervening.

" It does not seem to be suspected in Europe that a very advanced decorative art exists among the Maoris, both in New Zealand and in the Marquesas. The clever critic is mistaken when he takes all this for Papuan art!

" The Marquesan especially has an incomparable sense of decoration. Give him an object of any geometrical shape, even distorted, and he will succeed in making a harmonious whole without leaving the slightest break or incongruity. The basis of it is the human body or the face — above all, the face. Where one expected a strange geometrical figure, one is astonished to find a face. Always the same thing and yet never the same.

" Today no money could buy any of those beautiful objects in bone, tortoise-shell or iron-wood that they used to make. The gendarmerie have *stolen* them all and sold them to amateur collectors, and yet the administration has never thought for a moment of opening a museum in Tahiti for all this Oceanic art, a thing which it might so easily have done.

" Not one of these people, who call themselves well-informed, has ever had an idea of the value of the Marquesan artists. There is not a wife of the humblest official who would not exclaim on seeing

it: ' But this is horrible! It's barbarous! ' Barbarous! that's their cry.

" They are the people who mar any festivity in these countries with their out-of-date fashions, ridiculous from head. to foot, vulgar hips, tight-laced figures, sham jewellery, elbows that threaten or bulge like sausages. But they are white, and they carry their stomachs high.

" Those of the population who are not white are really elegant. Our critical gentleman is a long way out of it when he says with disdain: ' Negresses ' — unless it is I who have been mistaken in describing and drawing them.

" One man says: ' They are Papuans '; another: ' They are Negresses.' This is enough to give me serious doubts of my claims as an artist. Loti, you say? Thank you, that's very nice.

" Let us just determine the designation of this race, as I see it, and let us call it the Maori race, leaving it to someone else, more or less of a photographer, to describe and paint it later on with his more civilized and accurate art.

" I say ' really elegant ' and I mean it. Every woman makes her gown, plaits her hat, and trims it with ribbons in a way any Paris milliner might be proud of, arranges a bouquet with the taste of the boulevard de la Madeleine. Their handsome figure sways gracefully under the lace and muslin chemise. The hands that appear from their sleeves are essen-

tially aristocratic; their broad and powerful feet, unshod, will not trouble us for long, for it will soon be the boots that offend our eyes. Another thing in the Marquesas that sometimes offends the prudes is that all these girls smoke pipes — the calumet, no doubt, to those who are on the look-out for barbarism.

" Be this as it may, the Maori woman could never be dowdy or ridiculous, even if she tried, since she has within her that sense of decorative beauty which I admire in Marquesan art, after having studied it. But is it nothing but that? Does a pretty mouth count for nothing, with a smile that shows such beautiful teeth? They talk about Negresses! What nonsense!

" And that pretty breast with its pink buds that will not submit to the corset. What distinguishes the Maori woman from all others and often leads one to mistake her for a man is the proportions of her figure. A Diana the huntress with broad shoulders and narrow hips.

" However thin her arm may be, the bony structure is scarcely apparent, the lines are soft and supple. Have you noticed our Western girls at a ball, with gloves up to the elbow, skinny arms, all elbow, ugly in fact, with the forearm thicker than the upper arm?

" I say Western women advisedly, for the Maori's arm is the same as that of all Eastern women — only stronger.

" Again, have you noticed at the theatre the legs of the ballet-girls? Those enormous thighs (nothing but thighs), the huge knees, turned in. This is probably due to an exaggerated expansion of the joint of the femur. Whereas in the Eastern woman, and especially the Maori, the leg from hip to foot gives a beautifully straight line. The thigh is very pronounced, but not in its breadth, and this gives it a roundness and avoids that hollow which makes us compare some of our women to a pair of tweezers.

" To return to Marquesan art. This art has disappeared, thanks to the missionaries. In the judgment of the missionaries sculpture and decoration were fetishism, offensive to the God of the Christians.

" That was the whole thing, and the unhappy people have submitted.

" The younger generation, from the very cradle, chants the canticles in a French that nobody understands, recites the catechism, and then —

" Nothing — as you may well understand.

" If a young girl binds the flowers she has plucked into a pretty and artistic wreath and puts it on her head, Monseigneur is furious!

" Soon the Marquesan will be incapable of climbing a coconut-tree, incapable of going up the mountain for the wild bananas on which he might live. The child, kept at school, deprived of physical exercise, made to wear clothes (for decency's sake),

grows up delicate, unable to bear a night in the mountains. They have taken to wearing shoes, and their feet, now tender, will no longer be fit for rough paths or for crossing the pebbly beds of torrents.

" Thus we are witnessing the sad spectacle of the extinction of this race, now largely consumptive, with sterile loins and ovaries ruined by mercury."

The Marquesas did not possess the same economic interest for the French as did Tahiti; private persons were not numerous among the immigrants. The European life of the colony was dominated by a comparatively small number of officials and by the priests; as it often happened that months went by without a ship visiting the islands, and as the native population never gave trouble or did more work than was required of them, the course of daily life was calm and peaceful. Among themselves the natives lived in perfect amity. If anyone missed a hen or a pig, which, however, rarely happened, it was talked about today and forgotten tomorrow. Though jealousy was not unknown, it was still rather uncommon. In any case the natives were decidedly averse to applying to the authorities about their wrongs, and the latter on their side shut their eyes to everything that did not interfere with their own existence, or with the work of the Church among the Christian community of the islands. After the nervous agitation of his life in Tahiti, Gauguin here found peace

STILL LIFE

MARQUESAS, 1902

THE FLIGHT

and rest, which he sorely needed. The eczema in his legs and feet caused him great pain and aggravated his sleeplessness, and it was accompanied by frequent heart attacks and fits of morbid anxiety, which could only be quieted by alcohol and occasionally only with the aid of morphine.

" I have now resumed work fairly seriously, though still unwell. You can't imagine what a peaceful life I lead here in my solitude, entirely alone, surrounded by foliage. This is rest, and I needed it badly, away from all those officials in Tahiti. I congratulate myself daily on my decision; for another thing, life is cheaper here. I pay 60 centimes for an ordinary chicken, and now and then I buy a forty-pound pig for 6 or 7 francs. Wine and a few other imported articles are really the only things that cost money."

As usual after moving to a new place, Gauguin had to get accustomed to his surroundings before he could begin to work. And this time it took longer than ever before. Nearly six months had gone by without his having seriously handled a paint-brush. The delay was due not only to his need of a thorough rest, but to his new surroundings, which were in many ways different from those in Tahiti. He no longer lived in sight of the sea; his hut was situated in a fairly large and fertile valley, above which the mountains were boldly outlined against the sky.

The Marquesan women were taller, handsomer,

and lighter in colour; their bodies had a golden sheen which was very beautiful, and their firm, compact frames, even more than those of their Tahitian sisters, seemed carved out of a block. Whether walking, resting, or disrobing, there was a languid rhythm in all their movements, which was indescribably charming. It was only after long and careful study that he felt he really grasped them; they always kept at a certain distance, which relegated him to the position of an attentive observer, intimately as he imagined himself to know them. He often felt like one lying in wait to steal their souls, as they listened intently to the tales of ancient deeds from the lips of one of their elders — tales of the days when the warrior ate his fallen foe in order to secure his soul, but also because the Maori's flesh was good to eat, whereas that of the white man was not much — as the elder in question could declare from experience. It then became the duty of the dead man's relatives to get hold of the man who had eaten him, for then they could assimilate his soul as well as their kinsman's. That would give them power over their own clan and over its enemies.

The old man who enunciated these views looked significantly at Gauguin. " You are one of us, so I should like to eat you; but you are good, so I shall not have a chance. But I will put a taboo on you and your house, so that you will be protected against evil powers. The good powers will befriend you."

It happened now and then that on coming out on his veranda in the morning, Gauguin found a slaughtered hen hanging there. He looked round, trying to penetrate the thick bush that encircled the hut, and raised his hand in salute.

He had approached nearer to them, his kindly feeling for them was great, and his zest for work was awakened. The landscape was spread out before his eyes, its colours shining in the warm sunlight, and in the flickering shade of the thicket little Vaitauni in an unguarded moment was washing her linen. Her slender, compact body shone against the green foliage, which was flecked with patches of dark red. Was there perhaps a gendarme lurking in the bushes? If so, there would be a terrible fine to pay, or the price might be Vaitauni herself.

Thought gave a dramatic beauty to the picture, and nature acquired a majesty by the power it exercised over the minds of men, both for good and for evil. *Hoe!* Vaitauni whisked round, crouched down, and stared towards the clearing. She discovered him, drew herself up to her full height, and proudly approached his hut. The green shadows on her wet linen reproduced the soft lines of her body and brought out the warm glow of its colour. The smooth black hair, which gave a blue reflection in the strong light, held closely to the fine, simple shape of the head, spreading out on the neck and emphasizing the moulding and proud carriage of the round throat.

" *Vahiné*, I want to paint you."

" *Aita, tané*."

And other women came up, at first attracted by curiosity, later because they liked to visit this serious, silent man, who looked at them in a way they were so unused to, with an observant eye that was at the same time tender and intimate. And they liked to deck themselves when they came to see him, for he appreciated this. They soon discovered, too, that he was as fond of flowers as they were; they brought him bouquets and arranged them in his glass. And he painted these when his sufferings forced him to suspend more exacting tasks, as they very often did. In fact, the pains sometimes overcame him to such an extent, accompanied by recurring heart attacks, that he wished himself back in France, where he could receive better attention. And this longing was increased when the irregular palpitations gave him an instinctive presentiment of death. Moreover, his affairs at home seemed to be going better, so that, although no doubt Daniel was arranging everything for the best, there might be no harm in his taking a hand himself, which was difficult at this distance and with the irregular mail service.

And yet how calm and secure was his life in the islands! If only he could get well and wring the necks of the cursed priests and gendarmes, this would be the best place for him, since he no longer had a home in Europe and therefore no interest in a future

there. His eyes fell on the little morocco case in which he now kept the photographs of his children. Perhaps after all —

The thoughts chased each other in his mind, like sunshine and showers at home.

" *My dear Daniel,*

" The mail-boat for the Marquesas having taken a header into the sea, they have had the amusing idea of leaving us 85 days without mails, without news, without sugar or rice, etc. An obliging schooner has brought us a few letters, one from you, one from Fayet, two from Vollard. The last-named asks for some sculpture for himself. I have replied that he should apply to you. From the tone of his letter (I know the wily gentleman) I can guess that his business is looking up, as far as I am concerned, and that he finds an increasing demand for my production. It must be admitted that he is intelligent and that he is in touch with the *amateurs of good painting.* I am strongly recommending him to take the clay statue that you have — or perhaps it is still with Fayet — at a *price of 2,000 francs.* Although I must say I should have preferred it to form part of a serious collection, such as that of Fayet, even at 1,500 francs.

" The exhibition at Béziers' was no good. It can't be helped, and that's all there is to be said.

" As regards the picture which N— has on ap-

proval, *are you not afraid* that one day *he may be astonished at the price* when compared with those paid by Fayet? — these differences in price are a very delicate question. Naturally you must take this merely as an observation on my part, for I have told you before: *everything that you do will always be for the best.*

" By the way, Fayet writes that he hopes next year to arrange a very important exhibition of my works. Excellent!! I don't recommend a great number of canvases, but I want particular attention paid to their *quality* (fortunately you are there to see to this). If possible, the *big picture* which is at Bordeaux. Of the things Z— has I can see nothing but the *woodcarving*. If possible, the picture *Nevermore* from Delius. Nothing from Brittany (my work from Brittany is digested, whereas Tahiti has to be swallowed and sold). You know the public; they will say at once: ' What a pity he didn't stay in Brittany! ' You understand. — For that matter, who knows if I ought not to be there now? Because if I can't be cured of this chronic eczema in both feet, which gives me so much pain, I should be better for a change of air. Then I might settle in your part of the world, the south of France, where I could take a run into Spain in search of new subjects. Bullfights, Spaniards with their hair plastered with lard, it's been done, and done to death; all the same, it's queer how differently I imagine them.

" What a shame, though, to leave such a beautiful country as the Marquesas!

" From now on I am going to put aside anything I may get beyond the 350 francs from Vollard; this I can do without any trouble, for now I am not only paying my way but have a little to the good; besides, I can *live very well*, without *stinting myself*, on 250 francs, as living is a good deal cheaper here than in Tahiti.

" In his letter to me Fayet speaks of you and your talent, and how right he is! Beware of relying on your own opinion (one never knows oneself thoroughly). You can no longer put a figure on its feet? — let them lie down; that will give them a rest, and you too; and one fine day you will easily get them to stand up again.

" Meanwhile continue to enjoy life peacefully; the animal element in us is not to be despised in the way they try to make out. Those devils of Greeks, who understood everything, pictured Antæus recovering his strength by touching the earth. — The earth, that is our animality, believe me."

Gauguin enjoyed outward peace in the Marquesas, he was not worried by financial questions, life was simpler and easier here than in Tahiti, but at the same time his loneliness was greater. When the pains kept him awake at night and only stimulants could quiet his nerves by day, he often tried to bring life

into this loneliness. He saw himself and his work in relation to the development which had taken place in French art, and saw how he stood alone and how isolated his work appeared, since he had never allowed its fundamental thought to be affected by the social ideas of the time, which aimed at converting universal emotions into common property under some label or other.

In his painting, on the other hand, the fundamental idea was the assertion of the right of the individual to live his own life, and his purpose was to erect on this foundation a work which should have a meaning and a beauty capable of convincing. Many a time when his vision and his taste for work were impaired by illness, he would be seized by a misgiving that perhaps his powers would not last out until he had reached his goal. And in his solitude there was no voice to give him a word of encouragement.

With dimmed eyes and a throbbing heart he looked out over the valley, followed its undulations up towards the cliff, and paused at the huge white cross which stood on the edge of a plateau dominating the district with its cold and glaring outline against the face of the rock. It stood in the cemetery as a promise of eternal life in the bosom of the Church, but to him it was a terrible reminder of impotence and death.

Formerly the thought of death had never caused him pain; rather the contrary. But now it seemed

to be lying in wait to catch him unprepared before he had completed his work.

" I only ask for two years of health and not too many money worries, which now have too much of a hold on my nervous temperament, in order to attain to a certain maturity in my art. I feel that *I am right* in art, but shall I have strength to express it convincingly? In any case I shall have done my duty, and if my works do not last, at any rate the memory will persist of an artist who liberated painting from many of the faults of its academic past and from the delusions of Symbolism (another form of sentimentalism)."

The thought of going back to France now gave rise to feelings quite different from those which had accompanied his return in 1893. At that time he had thought himself strong enough to be able to assert himself with the aid of the personal character of his work and to break down the barriers which a civilized community always sets up against anything independent and unusual. But he had not reckoned with a new barrier that had been raised, compounded of a fresh and tenacious notion which went by the name of *l'Art nouveau*.

Now that he was possibly nearing his journey's end, his only thought was of simplifying and clarifying his art, so as to disengage it from the mysticism and the many misunderstandings that clung to it. And that clung no less to his life, which had merely

been a struggle to live in freedom without regard to conventions and prejudices.

" I have endeavoured to fight against all those parties which in every age assemble about a dogma, leading astray not only the painters, but also the connoisseurs. When will these people understand the meaning of the word ' Liberty '? "

A struggle which concerned not only himself but the whole of humanity, and which he felt sure would one day lead to the acknowledgment of the rights of the individual, when once class and sectarian feeling were played out, so that intellectual and cultural arrogance no longer had them to juggle with.

This game was still going on and was nowhere more flourishing than in the Marquesas, where a little band of Europeans in the name of civilization were trying forcibly to strangle the instincts of a proud and handsome primitive people, while playing with them at the same time as an outlet for their own private vices, for the satisfaction of which the despised Maori was not judged to be unsuitable.

By means of taxes and fines for the smallest delinquency the gendarmerie forced the natives to work for them and for the Church, and these naïve and easy-going people, who understood nothing of European duplicity, were far too ready to fall into the trap when the gendarmerie was in need of funds or the individual gendarme of a little entertainment. In the name of Liberty, Equality, and Fraternity a

veiled form of slavery was carried on, to which the Church gave its blessing, graciously accepting the offerings it entailed. But this revolted Gauguin both as a man and as a Frenchman. He saw with contempt how his own race dishonoured itself by its hypocrisy and ruthlessness, and he looked with infinite sorrow on the degradation of a beautiful and natural race, which was being driven out of existence, without submitting, without complaining, simply without understanding anything about it.

Seething with emotion he wrote to the colonial inspectors, who visited the Marquesas every eight months to investigate the affairs and administration of the islands. In preparation for their visit he gave them an unvarnished account of all he had witnessed. He had seen so much actual and palpable villainy and injustice committed against the natives that he had no difficulty in drawing up a defence of them and their existence and an indictment against the French colonial administration. He was a warm defender and a cold accuser.

" What a strange irony there is in this hypocritical regard for Liberty, Equality, Fraternity under the French flag when one sees it in the light of this revolting spectacle of men who are no longer anything but the objects of all sorts of extortions and are left to the mercy of the gendarme. And yet they are forced to shout: ' Long live the Governor, long live the Republic! '

" When the Fourteenth of July comes round, there will be 400 francs for distribution among them, whereas, besides their taxes, direct and indirect, they will have paid over 30,000 francs in fines.

" We colonists therefore consider this a dishonour to the French Republic, and you need not be surprised if some foreigner should say to you: ' I'm glad I'm not a Frenchman,' while the Frenchman will say: ' I wish the Marquesas belonged to America! '

" What do we ask, after all? That justice may be justice, not an empty word, but effectively, and that to achieve this we may have competent men of good feeling sent here to study the question on the spot and then to act with energy . . . in the full light of day.

" When the governors chance to pass this way they only come to take photographs, and when any respectable person ventures to address them, asking them to repair an injustice, he is treated as guilty of rudeness and deserving of punishment.

" That, gentlemen, is all I have to say to you. I do not know whether it will interest you, or whether you will say with Pangloss:

" ' Everything is for the best, in the best of all possible worlds.' "

The gendarmes were soon made to feel that a watchful eye was following their movements, even in the thickest bush. But they shrugged their shoulders — *O na tu*. It's only that mad painter, sick and

drunken too, they say, though he never shows it. On the other hand, you can see it by his pictures. He's no business of ours; even if the silly monkeys love their Koké and take his part, as he takes theirs, he won't catch us. They meant to pinch him before the inspectors arrived. What witnesses had he? The native interpreter would not dare to translate anything that went against the gendarmes; he could be coaxed and scared by turns — give him some drink on the sly and then threaten to report him. He could be fixed.

But when Gauguin came riding or driving along the road, clad in his *pareo*, with his cloak slung over his back and his cap drawn tightly about his skull, they bowed humbly with a guilty conscience in reply to his cold and silent salute. And this made them hate him. The subservience that is due to a sense of shame is hard to bear and not easily forgotten.

The other colonists on the island were either indifferent or wished to keep in with the gendarmes on account of liquor-smuggling. The Catholic mission saw in him a danger. Paul Vernier, the Protestant missionary, alone watched the silent and unapproachable man with profound admiration and respect, and he alone fully understood the value of the frank and confident look with which the natives met Gauguin.

But Vernier's own position was a lonely one in the colony, where he devoted himself entirely to the care

of the sick and those who needed his aid. It was with grave concern that he saw the signs of advancing illness in Gauguin's features. But from his conversations with the artist he had found that Gauguin never talked about himself, but only about his art and the Maoris. And he smiled indulgently when others spoke of the painter's inordinate egoism.

Gauguin made slow progress in his work; his illness kept him idle for many weeks whenever a few days' respite had allowed him to throw himself into it intently. His eyesight was impaired and unable to bear the strong light, and his hand was no longer so sure. And then the pains returned. He could only allay them by resorting to stimulants, which became more and more indispensable to him. The unproductive weeks grew longer and more frequent, the days of work fewer and shorter.

By the beginning of the year 1903 he could only move about with the greatest difficulty and could only paint for very brief spells; a snow landscape from Brittany stood on his easel. His memories overwhelmed him in his solitude, and he began to write — *Avant et Après*. Before he became an artist and human, and after.

" Stray notes without sequence, like dreams, like life itself, all made up of fragments. And, since many have borne a share in it, a love of beautiful things seen in the houses of others.

" Things that may appear childish when written,

sometimes for one's own pastime, sometimes in order to classify one's favourite ideas — though they may be foolish ones — distrusting a bad memory, and all of them leading to the vital centre of my art. For if a work of art were a work of chance, all these notes would be futile.

" I consider that the thought which may have guided my work, or a part of it, is connected, in some very mysterious way, with a thousand other thoughts, either my own or derived from others. I can recall days when my imagination strayed and I made long studies, often sterile, more often disturbing: a black cloud has appeared, darkening the horizon; confusion takes possession of my soul and I cannot see my way. But if in other hours of bright sunlight, with a clear mind, I have fastened upon some fact, some vision, something I have read, ought I not to preserve a brief record of it?

" Sometimes I have gone very far back, farther even than the horses of the Parthenon . . . as far as the good hobby-horse of my childhood.

" I have lingered with Corot's nymphs, dancing in the sacred groves of Ville-d'Avray.

" This is not a book."

All fugitive memories, which in all likelihood would never find a continuation in his life; the thread was to be severed, but the memories should be put on record, and his own place in them. There remained only his art; no doubt must be left as to its aim, nor

as to the conditions in which it had been produced. Conditions which had been largely brought about by the changing and often disastrous circumstances of his life and by many conflicting elements in his own nature.

Whether he was destined to stay in the islands or to return to France, the reminiscences of *Before and After* must be completed. He was to begin a new existence. Out here he could make no further progress in his art; he must go home, to find rest and peace.

And according to Daniel's last letter there was a hope that he would be able to find this rest and the medical care which he so sorely needed. It was now March, so he would reach home by the spring; all that troubled him now was the thought of abandoning his dear friends the natives to the mercy of the gendarmes.

A summons to appear in court recalled him forcibly to the present. He was charged by the lieutenant of gendarmes with having wrongfully accused this government official of breaches of duty. He knew the danger this charge involved. All those of his own race would be against him. The gendarme would declare to the judge — who knew nothing and had neither time nor inclination to familiarize himself with every case — that if these people, these bandits, were not treated sternly, all the whites would be murdered. Gauguin had espoused their cause, and all his allegations were derived from the lips of these

cannibals, who were incapable of uttering a word of honest French. He was a dangerous man. And Gauguin knew at the same time that he could expect no pity on account of being a sick man and scarcely able to drag himself before the court. And yet he had the firmest belief in the justice of his cause and lived in a terrible state of tension and excitement while awaiting the trial. So much so that when the case came up he entirely lost his self-control. He was found guilty and sentenced. This was the last straw.

" *My dear Daniel,*

" I send you three pictures which you will probably receive after your letter. Will you tell M. Fayet that this is a case of saving me? If he does not care for these pictures, let him choose others from those you have, or let him lend me 1,500 francs on any security he likes. This is why: I have just been the victim of a horrible piece of sharp practice. — Following on certain scandalous doings here in the Marquesas, I wrote to the Administrator, asking him to institute an inquiry. It had not occurred to me that the gendarmes were all in league with one another, that the Administrator would take the part of the Governor, and so on. Anyhow, the lieutenant demanded a prosecution, and a rascal of a judge, acting under the orders of the Governor and of a petty attorney whom I had treated rather roughly, sentenced me (press law of July '81), on account of a private

letter, to three months' imprisonment and a fine of
1,000 francs. I shall have to go to Tahiti to appeal.
How much is that going to cost me? — voyage,
board and lodging, and, above all, *lawyer's fees!!* It
means ruin and the complete break-up of my health.

"It will be said that all my life I have been con-
demned to fall, pick myself up, fall down again, etc.
All my old energy is disappearing day by day —

"So act as quickly as you can, and please say to
M. Fayet that I shall be eternally grateful to him. —

"Here is the mail at last: nothing yet from you.
Three mails have come in without Vollard writing
or sending me any money. At the moment he owes
me 1,500 francs, plus the balance on the pictures I
have sent him. This makes me a debtor for 1,400
francs to the Société Commerciale at the very moment when I have to ask them for more money to go
to Papeete, etc. I am very much afraid the bank will
refuse me, and then I shall be really in the soup. If
he is dead or has gone bankrupt, I hope you will have
been informed. All these worries and uncertainties
are *killing me.*"

Shortly after the decision of the court Gauguin
had to send for Vernier; he could no longer walk.
Vernier found him lying down, calmly smoking a
cigarette, but the pain he suffered was reflected in
his face. Both legs were swollen and inflamed with
eczema. After examining him Vernier proposed the

necessary treatment and offered to give it to him.
Gauguin declined; he would manage it himself. Instead he began to talk about his art and made some
references to his affair with the gendarme. And the
conversation calmed him. He smiled as Vernier took
his leave. He was alone again, but every morning his
native neighbour Tioka came to see him. Otherwise
an untrustworthy Chinese boy was his only attendant. He wished it so, was unwilling to trouble anyone
with his sufferings, would scarcely allow anyone to
see them. When about ten days later Vernier came
to see him again, he began at once to talk to him
about art. It seemed as though the thought of it eased
his pains and quieted his heart.

Early in the morning of May 8th Gauguin sent
Tioka to ask Vernier to come over. He complained of
violent pains all over. He had had two fainting-fits
during the night and was alarmed about them. He
soon changed the subject to Flaubert's *Salammbô*,
and an hour later he calmed down, telling Vernier
that he felt better now and there was no cause for
anxiety.

But at eleven o'clock the same morning the Chinese boy came running across to Vernier, crying out:
" Come at once! The white man is dead! " When
Vernier reached the hut, Tioka stood there weeping;
and on seeing the Protestant pastor he flung himself
upon his beloved friend and bit him in the thigh to
bring him back to life. But that had no effect, and

Vernier's efforts were also in vain. Gauguin was dead. Vernier laid him out on the couch. As he went away he heard Tioka's lament:

" *Na mate Koké. Na pete enate.*

" Gauguin is dead. We are lost."

INDEX

INDEX